Maud Howe Elliot

Art and Handicraft in the Woman's Building of the World's

Columbian Exposition

Vol. 1

Maud Howe Elliot

Art and Handicraft in the Woman's Building of the World's Columbian Exposition
Vol. 1

ISBN/EAN: 9783337371104

Printed in Europe, USA, Canada, Australia, Japan

Cover: Foto ©Thomas Meinert / pixelio.de

More available books at **www.hansebooks.com**

ART AND HANDICRAFT

IN THE

𝕸oman's 𝕭uilding

OF THE

WORLD'S COLUMBIAN EXPOSITION

CHICAGO, 1893

EDITED BY

MAUD HOWE ELLIOTT

WITH SPECIAL ARTICLES BY

MRS. POTTER PALMER, MRS. JULIA WARD HOWE, MISS S. T. HALLOWELL, MRS. CANDACE
WHEELER, MISS ALICE C. MORSE, MRS. ELIZABETH W. PERRY, MRS. LOUISA HOPKINS,
MRS. HENRY RICHARDS, MRS. FREDERICK P. BELLAMY, MRS. EDNA D.
CHENEY, MRS. JAMES P. EAGLE, MRS. FRANCES B. CLARKE,
MRS. GEORGE B. DUNLAP, MRS. MAUD HOWE ELLIOTT
AND
THE DUCHESS OF VERAGUA, THE PRINCESS M. SCHAHOVSKOY, THE COUNTESS OF ABERDEEN,
THE BARONESS BURDETT-COUTTS, THE BARONESS THORBURG RAPPE, MME. PÉGARD,
FRAU PROFESSORIN HASELOWSKY, MME. QUELLENAU, MME. ONHOLM, MRS.
BEDFORD-FENWICK, MRS. E. CRAWFORD, MME. EVA MARRIOTTI

𝕴llustrated

—

CHICAGO AND NEW YORK :

RAND, McNALLY & COMPANY.

1894.

WOMAN'S BUILDING. DESIGNED BY SOPHIA G. HAYDEN. UNITED STATES.

PUBLISHERS' PREFACE.

The World's Columbian Exposition has afforded woman an unprecedented opportunity to present to the world a justification of her claim to be placed on complete equality with man.

The broad fact that able and earnest women from all quarters of the globe organized for the purpose of gathering evidence and demanding a hearing by the court of assembled nations is generally known. The following pages—written by women eminent as pleaders in the cause—tell eloquently of the detail of their procedure and of the results so far attained.

That their labors will immediately eventuate in the full realization of their hopes can not with reason be expected, but that their efforts have revealed the possession of unsuspected powers, and will disperse the mists of ignorant prejudice that at present cloud the question, can not be doubted.

The publishers hail with pleasure the opportunity that the issuance of this volume affords them of adding to the light, and perhaps of hastening the coming of the day when woman will be emancipated from restraints imposed upon her by a worn-out conventionalism absurdly unsuited to our times and conditions.

The illustrations in the original edition of this work were prepared and made by Boussod, Valadon & Co. (successors to Goupil & Co.), in Paris ; and the illustrations made by Rand, McNally & Co. appear in the present edition on pages 26, 32, 41, 42, 69, 70, 77, 78, 95, 96, 108, 110, 123, 124, 131, 132, 144, 146, 159, 160, 186, 188, 197, 198, 223, 224, 254, 256, 280, 282, 296, and 298.

LAGOON LAGOON

LANDING

EAST

Ground Plan:

LOGGIA — LOGGIA

GERMANY

WOMEN'S TOILET — WOMEN'S TOILET

AUSTRIA — INDIA — BRAZIL

AMERICAN APPLIED ARTS

PAPER FLOWERS

PROCESS ROOM

EDUCATIONAL ROOM

ENGLISH PAVILION

SMITHSONIAN

INDIAN AND AFRICAN

INVENTIONS

BELGIUM

GERMANY — FRANCE — SPAIN

CEYLON

NORTH

VOTING BOOTH

CORRIDOR

LOAN EXHIBITION

ROTUNDA

CORRIDOR

SPAIN

SIAM — SWEDEN

JAPAN

RUSSIA

DRESS MAKERS

CORN PALACE

STAINED GLASS

VOTER

AUSTRIA — ENGLAND

AMERICA — SPAIN

ELEVATOR — CLOAK ROOM — GOOD ROADS — FIGURES

MÉXICO

ITALY

IRISH & SCOTCH INDUSTRIES

AUSTRALIA

WOMEN'S TOILET

SALES ROOM

SALES ROOM

CHECK ROOM & GUIDES

BUREAU OF INFORMATION P. O. & TEL.

SCIENTIFIC

SCIENTIFIC

MEN'S TOILET

ENGLAND

LOGGIA — LOGGIA

FRANCE

WEST

GROUND PLAN WOMAN'S BUILDING.

Gallery Plan:

EAST

RETIRING

PLATFORM

RETIRING

BALCONY — BALCONY

BOARD OF LADY MANAGERS

MRS. PALMER'S ROOM

WOMEN'S — WOMEN'S

PRIVATE ROOM

JAPANESE ROOM

CALIFORNIA ROOM

CINCINNATI ROOM

KENTUCKY ROOM

SUPT. OF BLDG.

PRIVATE ROOM

OFFICE

ASSEMBLY ROOM

CORRIDOR

NORTH

MEN

CORRIDOR

ELEVATOR

CORRIDOR

CORRIDOR
NEW YORK LOAN EXH.

ORGANIZATION ROOM

MODEL

CORN

KITCHEN

PANTRY

COMMITTEE ROOM

FOREIGN COMMIS.

RECORD ROOM

LIBRARY

RECORD ROOM

ENG. SCHOOL FOR NURSES

AFRO-AMER. EXH.

INDIAN EXH.

BALCONY — BALCONY

WEST

GALLERY PLAN WOMAN'S BUILDING.

CONTENTS.

LIST OF ILLUSTRATIONS.

NOTE.—The illustrations in the following list are of objects displayed in the Woman's Building. The particular section in which an exhibit is to be found is indicated by the name of the country following the title of each illustration.

ADDITIONAL ILLUSTRATIONS IN THIS EDITION.

MRS. SUSAN G. COOKE.
Secretary Board of Lady Managers.

MRS. V. C. MEREDITH,
Vice-Chairman Executive Committee,
and Chairman of Committee on Awards.

MRS. POTTER PALMER,
President Board of Lady Managers.

MRS. RUSSELL B. HARRISON,
Vice-President at Large.

MRS. JOHN A. LOGAN,
Vice-Chairman Committee on Ceremonies.

PROMINENT OFFICIALS OF THE BOARD OF LADY MANAGERS.

MRS. EDWIN C. BURLEIGH,
Second Vice-President.

MRS. RALPH TRAUTMANN,
First Vice-President.

MRS. CHARLES PRICE,
Third Vice-President.

MISS K. L. MINOR,
Fourth Vice-President.

MRS. BERIAH WILKINS,
Fifth Vice-President.

MRS. SUSAN R. ASHLEY,
Sixth Vice-President.
(Resigned.)

MRS. FLORA BEALL GINTY,
Seventh Vice-President.

MRS. MARGARET BLAINE
SALISBURY,
Eighth Vice-President.

VICE-PRESIDENTS OF THE BOARD OF LADY MANAGERS.

HER IMPERIAL HIGHNESS
MARIE THERESE,
President Imperial Ladies' Com-
mission, Austria.

MRS. SKOUZIS,
President of the Syllogue, Athens,
Greece.

MRS. SCHEPLER-LETTE,
Germany.

MRS. GEN. VISCHNEGRADSKY,
President Imperial Ladies' Com-
mission, Russia.

MME. CARNOT,
President Ladies' Committee.
France.

FOREIGN LADY COMMISSIONERS.

ART AND HANDICRAFT IN THE
WOMAN'S BUILDING.

THE GROWTH OF THE WOMAN'S BUILDING.

THE authorization of a Board of Lady Managers by Congress came by the natural process of evolution, and was the direct result of the good work done by women at the Centennial Exhibition in Philadelphia and the succeeding Cotton Centennial at New Orleans.

In Philadelphia the Woman's Commission, led by Mrs. Gillespie, worked long and earnestly, not only to bring together the exhibits shown in the Woman's Department, but to raise the funds necessary to build the woman's pavilion and to provide the opening chorus, which was composed for the occasion by Wagner, and sung by a thousand children's voices. The creation of the Department of Public Comfort, which grew to be of immense value and importance, was the suggestion of the women, though the men adopted and enlarged upon it. The work done was heroic, and the leaders deserved to be immortalized for the tremendous results brought about with so little outside aid.

In New Orleans, at the Cotton Centennial, Mrs. Julia Ward Howe, aided by one woman commissioner from each State and Territory, did a grand work. When the women's exhibit was brought together in New Orleans, it was found that the Exposition Company had not funds enough to enable the managers to fit up their department and show their goods. Mrs. Howe then made a direct appeal to Congress, through some of her friends who were members of that body, and the sum of $15,000 was voted to the Woman's Department in order to help them out of their uncomfortable situation. The valuable work done by these two organizations of women had prepared the public mind so thoroughly for the coöperation of women in exposition work that when the matter

2 (17)

WATER-COLOR. MADELAINE LEMAIRE. FRANCE.

was brought before the World's Fair Committee of Congress, Mr. Springer of Illinois willingly inserted the clause authorizing the creation of the board of women, and championed it in the committee and before the House, where it met with no serious opposition.

The Board of Lady Managers was created by an Act of Congress, Section 6 of which reads as follows: "And said Commission is authorized and required to appoint a Board of Lady Managers of such number and to perform such duties as may be prescribed by said Commission. Said board may appoint one or more members of all committees authorized to award prizes for exhibits which may be produced in whole or in part by female labor."

Upon the assembling of the Board of Lady Managers in Chicago, we found that the first important duty to be settled was whether the work of women at the Fair should be shown separately or in conjunction with the work of men under the general classifications. This was a burning question, for upon this subject every one had strong opinions, and there was great feeling on both sides, those who favored a separate exhibit believing that the extent and variety of the valuable work done by women would not be appreciated or comprehended unless shown in a building separate from the work of men. On the other hand, the most advanced and radical thinkers felt that the exhibit should not be one of *sex*, but of *merit*, and that women had reached the point where they could afford to compete side by side with men, with a fair chance of success, and that they would not *value* prizes given upon the sentimental basis of sex.

Both in Philadelphia and New Orleans the plan of separate exhibits had been carried out as well as possible; but in both cases the friends of women were disappointed by the meager showing made when the work done by women *alone* was separated, and they were not credited with the immense amount, both in variety and volume, which women had done *in conjunction with men*.

From the farm the dairy products went into the general exhibit, presumably as men's work. The interesting and unusually attractive showing of the bee and silk-worm industries, although prepared largely by women, went also into the general classification; and so with the thousand and one articles made in the factories of the world by men and women working conjointly; for women's distinctive part could not be separated without destroying the finished article.

In *our* body the vote on this question did not come up directly,

MINIATURE—"TOILET OF VENUS." MME. HERVÉ. FRANCE.

but indirectly, when it was decided, and I think wisely, that there should be no separate exhibit, but that each manufacturer should be expected to state whether his exhibit was in whole or part the work of women; and that we should have some device indicating this fact placed thereon, so that all who go through the Exposition and are at all interested in this matter can easily see a statement of the facts.

Our request to the Committee of Installation to put the necessary questions in the entry blanks, then being prepared to send to proposed exhibitors, was immediately granted, and almost all of the manufacturers who sent in their applications for space answered our questions, the first being: " Was this article produced wholly or in part by the work of women?" The affirmative answer to this question entitles us to members on the juries of award—a most important privilege for the protection of women's interests, which was conferred upon us by Congress. A good illustration was given of the lack of appreciation of the universality of woman's work in the world, when I asked one of the members of the Board of Control, at the time they were prescribing our duties, how many representatives we might have on the juries which would pass upon exhibits that were wholly or in part the work of women. His reply was that we might appoint all the members of those juries; that they were perfectly willing for us to name the entire jury that was to award prizes in departments where women's work was to be judged. This was so overwhelming, that I modestly insisted that we name only one-half of such juries, as otherwise, though I did not tell him so, we should have had the appointing of all the members of all the juries of the Exposition, except in very few of the departments of classification.

The desire of the Board of Lady Managers is to present a complete picture of the condition of women in every country of the world at this moment, and more particularly of those women who are bread-winners. We wish to know whether they continue to do the hard, wearing work of the world at prices which will not maintain life, and under unhealthy conditions; whether they have access to the common schools and to the colleges, and after having taken the prescribed course are permitted graduating honors; whether the women, in countries where educational facilities are afforded them, take a higher stand in all the active industries of life as well as in intellectual pursuits; how large the proportion is of those who have shown themselves capable of taking honors in the colleges to which they are admitted, etc.

MARBLE BUST OF PRINCESS OBOLENSKY. PRINCESS M. SCHAHOVSKOY. RUSSIA.

We aim to show, also, the new avenues of employment that are constantly being opened to women, and in which of these they are most successful by reason of their natural adaptability; what education will best fit them for the new opportunities awaiting them, and to answer a host of kindred questions.

After a long period of inaction the enrollment of foreign women was rapidly effected, and we are now possessed of the most powerful organization that has ever existed among women, having official committees, created by government and supported by government funds, coöperating with us in England, France, Italy, Germany, Spain, Austria, Russia, Belgium, Holland, Sweden, Norway, Greece, Siam, Japan, Algeria, Cape Colony, Cuba, Mexico, Nicaragua, the Argentine Republic, Jamaica, Ceylon, Brazil, Colombia, Ecuador, Venezuela, Panama, and the Sandwich Islands.

The members of the English committee, under the patronage of the Queen, and of which the Princess Christian is president, have been chosen with singular discretion. Each chairman is a power in herself, as well as perfect mistress of her own line of work; and all are enthusiastically following the leadership of their much-loved president. To give an indication of the strength and efficiency of this committee, I need only mention such names as the Duchess of Abercorn, the Marchioness of Salisbury, the Countess of Aberdeen, Lady Henry Somerset, Lady Brassey, Baroness Burdett-Coutts, Lady Knutsford, Lady Jeune, Mrs. Bedford-Fenwick, and Mrs. Fawcett.

In France Madame Carnot accepted the active presidency of the committee. She secured committees of the most earnest, influential, and competent women to second her own efforts.

Italy was almost the first to announce its committee, under the special patronage of Queen Margherita, who is personally directing the work, and who will send her marvelous collection of historical laces, some of which date back 1,000 years before Christ, having been taken from Egyptian and Etruscan tombs. They are both personal and crown property, and have never before left Italy. This royally generous response to our appeal was doubly welcome, for it came when diplomatic relations between the two countries were suspended, and it was intended as a special mark of friendship. Accompanying this lace exhibit is a collection of the work of the Italian women of to-day, a prominent feature of which is the lace made by the peasant women in the societies organized by, and under the direction of, the queen. This exhibit will be one of the noted features of our building.

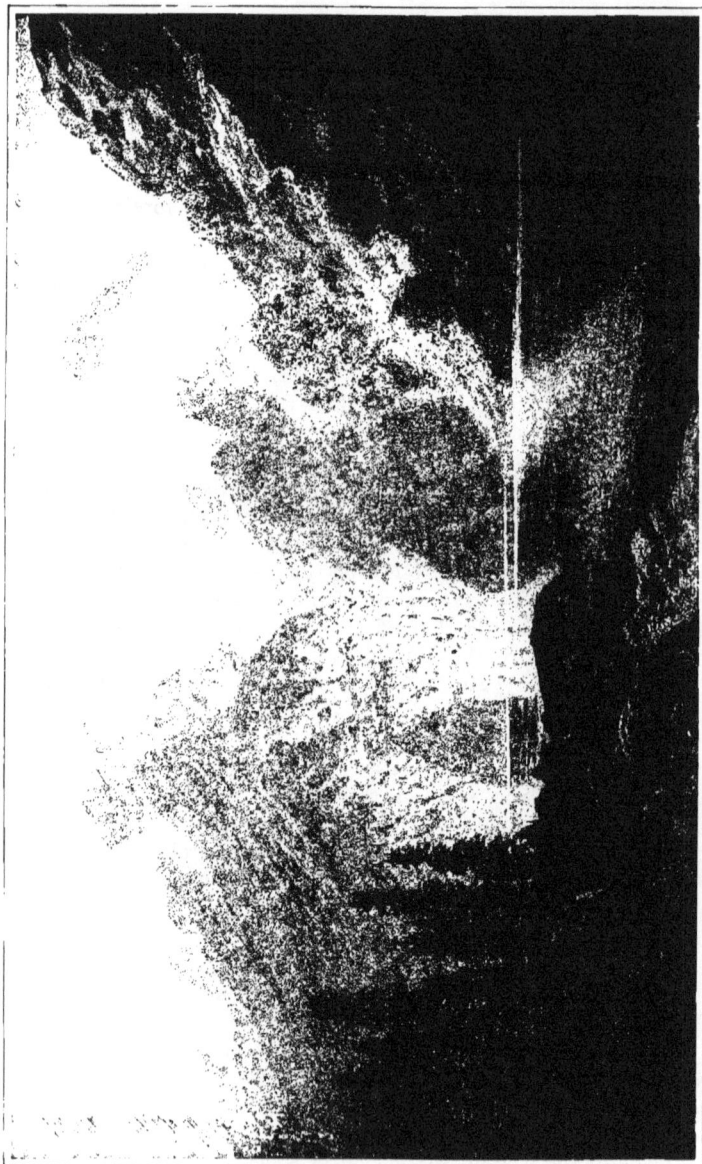

OIL PAINTING—LANDSCAPE. FRAULEIN VON KENDELL. GERMANY.

Russia, which has a committee organized by the Empress herself, sends its remarkable laces and embroideries, and many curious national costumes, which are very picturesque and attractive, both in color and design.

Japan at first hesitated, and refused to appoint a committee, but M. de Guerville had the good fortune to be permitted to give his lecture before the Emperor and Empress of Japan, and so interested the latter that she consented to become the head of a committee of ladies with whom we are now in active correspondence.

From parts of South America we shall rely mainly upon the kindly coöperation of the Latin-American department, which will send us such native work as can be spared from its own rich and varied collection. Although we have coöperating committees there, they have as yet made no definite reports as to what we may expect from them.

Madame Diaz has most kindly coöperated with us, and has offered for our building, in addition to other novel attractions, an orchestra of Mexican girls in rich costumes, who will play the national Mexican airs.

It will be seen that the names on our foreign committees represent not only royalty and the influence of government, but include also many women who have risen to the positions which they occupy by their own unaided talents, who, without titles or wealth to assist them, are recommended only by their evident ability to carry on the important lines of work intrusted to their hands.

The powerful organization which we have secured extends around the world, and stands with perfect solidarity for the purpose of serving the interests of our sex and making the industrial conditions easier for them. We have such an organization as has never before existed of women for women. That this work is needed is evidenced by the pathetic answers from some of the countries where our invitation has been declined. For instance, a letter received from the government of Tunis states that a commission of women can not be formed in that country, because local prejudice will not allow the native women to take part in public affairs. Syrian correspondents write that it will be impossible to secure the official appointment of a committee of women in that country, as custom prevents women from taking hold of such work, and the government will lend no aid; but that an effort will be made to send a small exhibit, unofficially. Other oriental countries make the same reports—no schools; women not intelligent enough to undertake the work; public prejudice, etc. It seems incredible

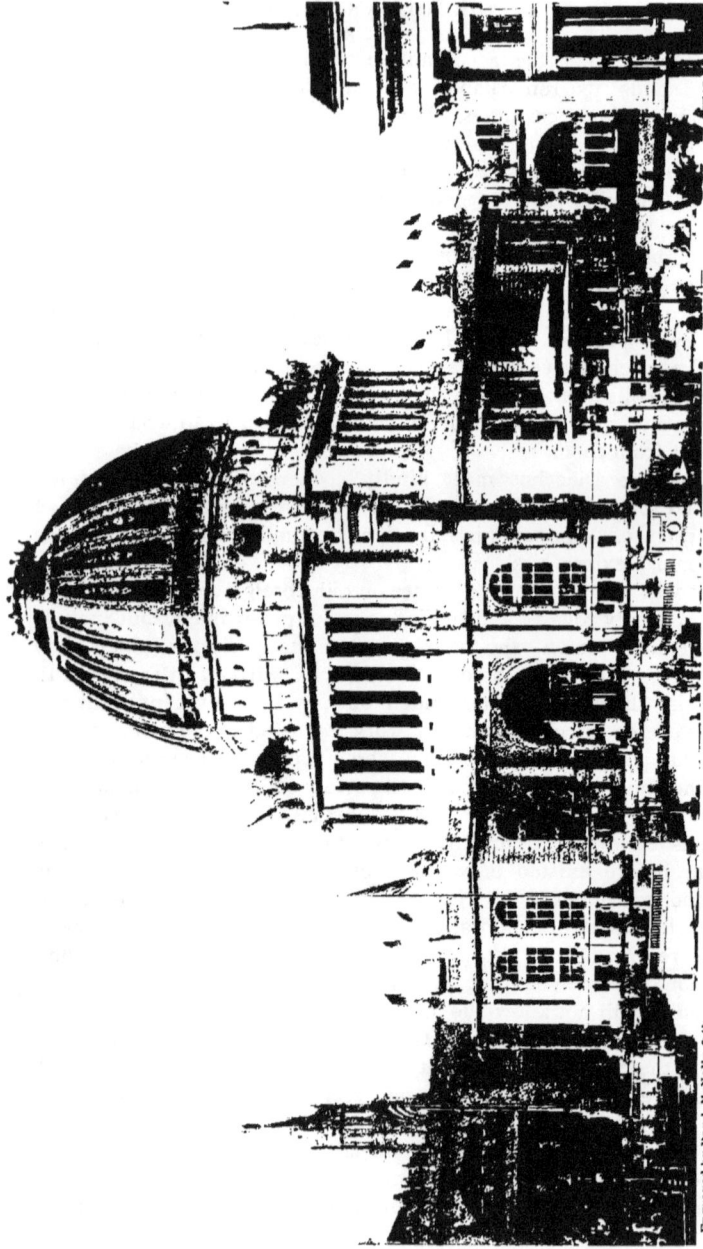

ADMINISTRATION BUILDING.

SIZE, MAIN BODY, 100 x 100 FEET; PAVILIONS, 84 x 84 FEET; HEIGHT OF DOME, 275 FEET. ARCHITECT, MR. RICHARD M. HUNT. COST, $450,000.

Engraved by Rand, McNally & Co.

that the governments of these countries would be willing to make admissions which reflect so much upon themselves, or that they would allow these shameful conditions to continue. The oppressive bonds laid upon women, both by religion and custom, are in some cases so strong as to be insurmountable, probably, during the present generation. A lady eminent for her work on behalf of the women of India, has informed me that the difficulty in doing anything for them is their absolute mental inactivity and their lack of desire to change their condition; they are so bound by the prevailing laws of caste and the prejudices that exist, that they have no wish for different surroundings; the desire for something better must be created before anything can be done to help them.

We have the hopeful fact to record, however, that even where the night has seemed the darkest, we have received letters from native women, to whom the dawn of a brighter day is visible, showing a full comprehension of the situation and an awakened intelligence. These women are working in their feeble way to send us, unofficially, such an exhibit as they can get together, notwithstanding official refusals. It is unfortunate that we can not hope to have women from the Orient present in large numbers at the Exposition, so that they might profit by its civilizing influences.

When our building was planned, we thought with some anxiety of the difficulty we would experience in getting creditable objects to fill so vast a space, but now we find that a building four or five times as large would have been inadequate. I now feel sure that notwithstanding the disappointments to exhibitors, this is a benefit to the quality of the collection, for such a vigorous process of elimination has been required in order to bring the exhibits within the bounds assigned, that it has resulted in the exclusion of all but the most desirable and attractive objects.

The moment of fruition has arrived. Hopes which for more than two years have gradually been gaining strength and definiteness have now become realities. The Exposition has opened its gates. On the occasion of the formal opening of the Woman's Building the Board of Lady Managers was singularly fortunate in having the honor of welcoming distinguished official representatives of many of the able foreign committees, and of the State boards which have so effectively coöperated with it in accomplishing results now disclosed to the world. We have traveled together a hitherto untrodden path, have been subjected to tedious delays, and overshadowed by dark clouds which threatened disaster to our enterprise. We have been obliged to march with peace offerings

OIL PAINTING—"A VISION." Frau Bieber Bohm. Germany.

in our hands, lest hostile motives be ascribed to us. Our burdens have been greatly lightened, however, by the spontaneous sympathy and aid which have reached us from women in every part of the world, and which have proved an added incentive and inspiration.

When our invitation asking coöperation was sent to foreign lands, the commissioners already appointed generally smiled doubtfully, and explained that their women were doing nothing; that they would not feel inclined to help us, and in many cases stated that it was not the custom of their country for women to take part in any public effort; that they only attended to their social duties, drove in the parks, etc. But as soon as these ladies received our message, sent in a brief and formal letter, the free-masonry among women proved to be such that it needed no explanation; they understood at once the possibilities. Strong committees were immediately formed of women having large hearts and brains— women who can not selfishly enjoy the ease of their own lives without giving a thought to their helpless and wretched sisters.

Our unbounded thanks are due to the exalted and influential personages who became, in their respective countries, patronesses and leaders of the movement inaugurated by us to represent what women are doing. They entered with appreciation into our work for the Exposition, because they saw an opportunity—which they gracefully and delicately veiled behind the magnificent laces forming the central objects in their superb collections—to aid their women by opening new markets for their wares.

This was the earnest purpose of their majesties the Empress of Russia and Queen of Italy, both so noted for the progressive spirit they have displayed in promoting the welfare of the women under their kindly rule. They have sent large collections of the work of peasant women, through organizations which exist under their patronage for selling their handiwork.

The committee of Belgian ladies was kind enough to take special pains to comply with our request for statistics concerning the industries and condition of women, notwithstanding the fact that the collecting of statistics is not in Europe so popular as with us. It has sent complete reports, attractively prepared in the form of monographs and charts, giving details which have been secured only by great personal effort. Such figures have never before been obtained in that country, and the committee itself is surprised at the great amount of novel and valuable information it has succeeded in presenting.

Her Majesty the Queen of England has kindly sent an exhibit of the work of her own hands, with the message that while she usually feels no interest in expositions, she gives this special token of sympathy with the work of the Board of Lady Managers because of its efforts for women. That the English committee has included in its exhibit and in its catalogue a plea for the higher education of women is in itself a significant fact.

Her Majesty the Queen of Siam has sent a special delegate with directions that she put herself under our leadership and learn what industrial and educational advantages are open to women in other countries, so that Siam may adopt such measures as will elevate the condition of her women.

The Exposition will thus benefit women, not alone by means of the material objects brought together, but there will be a more lasting and permanent result through the interchange of thought and sympathy among influential and leading women of all countries, now for the first time working together with a common purpose and an established means of communication. Government recognition and sanction give to these committees of women official character and dignity. Their work has been magnificently successful, and the reports which will be made of the conditions found to exist will be placed on record as public documents among the archives of every country.

We rejoice in the possession of this beautiful building, in its delicacy, symmetry, and strength. We honor our architect and the artists, who have given not only their hands but their hearts and their genius to its decoration.

The eloquent president of the Commission last October dedicated the great Exposition to humanity. We dedicate the Woman's Building to an elevated womanhood, knowing that by so doing we shall best serve the cause of humanity.

To serve as a permanent record of the many rare and beautiful objects now gathered in the Woman's Building, which will so soon be scattered to the four corners of the earth, this illustrated volume has been prepared. We greatly regret that lack of time and space has prevented our doing complete justice to the achievements of our sex, but hope that what has been accomplished may prove of service as a basis for future work.

BERTHA HONORÉ PALMER.

MARBLE STATUE—"SPRING." Mme. L. Contan. France.

Engraved by Rand, McNally & Co.

THE MANUFACTURES AND LIBERAL ARTS BUILDING. FROM ACROSS THE LAGOON; VIEWED FROM THE NORTHWEST.

THE BUILDING AND ITS DECORATION.

THE great work of the world is carried on by those inseparable yoke-mates man and woman, but there are certain feminine touches in the spiritual architecture which each generation raises as a temple to its own genius, and it is as a record of this essentially feminine side of human effort that the Woman's Building is dedicated.

In the dread art of war the male element of the race asserts itself alone. In its antithesis, the art of peace, woman is paramount. We are yoke-fellows, equal and indivisible, tugging and straining at the load of humanity which we must drag a few paces onward ere our work is done. On the outskirts of the throng of tireless workers there are a few men and women who, when the heat and stress of the day are over, climb to the hill-tops, and looking into the mute heavens read the promise of the coming day. A generation ago the seers of our race foretold two great things: a material growth and prosperity, the like of which the world has never seen; a mastery of electricity, that most potent of man's friendly genii, and a great city through which the traffic of the world should roll, one of the strongholds of the earth—all this the voice of the male seer foretold from his tower, and much more.

A clearer, sweeter prophecy went forth from the tower where the wise women watched the signs of the times: " Woman the acknowledged equal of man; his true helpmate, honored and beloved, honoring and loving as never before since Adam cried, ' The woman tempted me and I did eat.' "

We have eaten of the fruit of the tree of knowledge and the Eden of idleness is hateful to us. We claim our inheritance, and are become workers, not cumberers of the earth.

Twenty years ago to be called strong-minded was a reproach which brought the blood to the cheek of many a woman. To-day there are few of our sisters who do not prefer to be classed among strong-minded rather than among weak-minded women. The battle has been fought out, and the veterans who have been wounded and scarred with that cruelest weapon of ridicule, smile

DECORATION OF NORTH TYMPANUM—"PRIMITIVE WOMAN." MARY FAIRCHILD MACMONNIES. UNITED STATES.

to see how easily we assume the position which they gave the glory of their youth to win for us. We honor these women and have written their names in golden letters for all the world to see and salute in our Hall of Honor.

To see the work of woman at the World's Fair we must go through every department of human ingenuity, for there is scarcely one of these where woman's hand has not done a share of the work. The work of man and woman, like their interests, is one and indivisible.

In welcoming the visitor to our building, we would say: "Enter here for a space; sit in our library and rest your eyes with its soft colors; pace through our Hall of Honor and understand the spirit in which it is raised; leave criticism upon the threshold as you enter. Our salutation is, 'Peace be with you.' May your answer be, 'And with you be peace.'"

When I first wandered through the courts of this miraculous city, which has arisen as if by magic out of the desolate borderland between the prairie and the lake, I was moved, as rarely ever before, by the work of man's hand. I have stood upon the edge of the Egyptian desert and gazed with questioning eyes upon the mighty sphinx. I have seen the glories of the Acropolis and knelt at the shrine of the Greek, but neither of these superlative legacies of the past impressed me more than did this prophecy of the future. For the first time in the history of our nation, the spirit of art has asserted itself, and triumphs over its handmaidens, commerce and manufacture. The beauties of the Athens of Pericles, the Rome of Augustus, are indeed recalled by what we see, but a new art is foretold, whose ruins will one day be honored as we honor the classic fragments of Greece and Rome today. Comparison is nowhere more odious than where all is excellent; in my own thought our building stands on its own merits, and yet it bears comparison with all the rest, and loses nothing by it. There may be others which have qualities which it lacks. It borrows beauty from its august neighbors and from its mirrored reflection in the lagoon, but it lends as much as it receives, and the winged temple is joyfully restful to eyes wearied with much gazing. A work of art is precious in so far as it expresses the personality of its creator. Architecture is one of the arts most subservient to use, and a building should not only express the genius of the architect but the purpose to which it is dedicated. How well the architects of the great Gothic churches understood this law. No other form of religious architecture expresses so exalted a spirituality as theirs. The aspiring lines, the upspringing arches of the great Gothic cathedrals lead the eyes upward to the sky; the mind to reflection and aspiration. Our building is essentially feminine in character; it has the qualities of reserve, delicacy, and refinement. Its strength is veiled in grace; its beauty is gently impressive; it does not take away the breath

DECORATION OF SOUTH TYMPANUM.—"MODERN WOMAN." MARY CASSATT. UNITED STATES.

with a sudden passion of admiration, like some of its neighbors, but it grows upon us day after day, like a beloved face whose beauty, often forgotten because the face is loved for itself, now

DECORATIVE PANEL—"THE WOMEN OF PLYMOUTH."
LUCIA FAIRCHILD. UNITED STATES.

and again breaks upon us with all the charm of novelty. I came upon our building suddenly one early morning, when the mist-curtain was rolling away under a crisp breeze and an ardent sun. My heart leaped to a more generous measure. I drew my breath quickly. It seemed to me that I should always see it as then, peerless, shining, a fair temple to that which is essentially feminine in human life. The next day I hurried to my work within its doors with a single thought, that it was well and conveniently arranged for my purpose; but in the coming years I shall see our building in all its beauty as I saw it on that never-to-be-forgotten morning.

DECORATIVE PANEL—"ARCADIA."
AMANDA BREWSTER SEWELL. UNITED STATES.

The Woman's Building was planned by Miss Sophia Hayden of Boston, a graduate of the Massachusetts School of Technology, of the class of 1890. A national competition of designs by women resulted in the choice of Miss Hayden's plans. The site is admirably chosen from an artistic and practical standpoint. The building stands between the Horticultural Hall and the Bureau of Public

Comfort, directly adjacent to the Sixtieth Street entrance of the Fair. The nearest station of the suburban railway may be reached in a two minutes' walk.

Nothing is more significant of the difference in woman's position in the first and the latter half of our century than the fact that none of the eminent writers who have commented upon Miss Hayden's work have thought to praise it by saying that it looks like a man's work. Marian Evans and Aurore Dupin found it necessary to cloak their womanhood under the *noms de plume* of George Eliot and George Sand. Rosa Bonheur found it convenient to wear man's attire while visiting the Parisian stock-yards in order to study the animals for her great pictures. At that time the highest praise that could be given to any woman's work was the criticism that it was so good that it might be easily mistaken for a man's. To-day we recognize that the more womanly a woman's work is the stronger it is. In Mr. Henry Van Brunt's appreciative account of Miss Hayden's work, the writer points out that it is essentially feminine in quality, as it should be. If sweetness and light were ever expressed in architecture, we find them in Miss Hayden's building. Every line expresses elegance, grace, harmony.

The building is in the style of the villas of the Italian Renaissance. It is 388 feet long, 199 feet wide, and 70 feet high. It is divided into two stories, which are clearly indicated by the lines of the exterior. The most important feature required of the architect was the Hall of Honor, which forms the middle of the structure. This is a noble apartment, rising to the full height of the building, surrounded by a lower two-story structure forming the four facades, and containing the minor halls and offices required for committee and exhibition rooms. At the second story a corridor surrounds the hall, treated in the way of a cloister, with graceful arches springing from well-proportioned columns. Looking at the building from the water side, we have a central entrance and a pavilion at each end connected by an arcade. The main entrance has three arches and is surmounted by a loggia inclosed by a colonnade, over which rises the pediment. The loggia connects with a balcony, which runs from the central entrance to the pavilions and is enriched with pilasters of the Corinthian order. Over the pavilions are roof-gardens, surrounded by an open screen of light Ionic columns, with caryatides over the loggia below. The ornamentation which outlines the arches and enriches the exterior is most appropriate. The finely modeled pediment and the eight typical groups of sculpture surmounting the open screen around the roof-

garden are in harmony with the purity, simplicity, and dignity of
the building, proving that Miss Rideout, the young Californian
sculptor of these charming groups, worked in perfect sympathy
with the architect.

The group represented in the pediment typifies woman's work
in the various walks of life. The central figure is full of spirit and

DECORATIVE PANEL—"THE REPUBLIC'S WELCOME TO HER DAUGHTERS."
ROSINA EMMET SHERWOOD. UNITED STATES. (Copyrighted.)

charm. In one hand she holds a myrtle wreath; in the other, the
scales of justice. On her right, we find Woman the Benefactor;
and on her left, the Woman, the Artist and Littérateur. The
figures are modeled in very high relief, and the whole work has an

infinitely joyous and hopeful quality. This is equally true of the winged groups, which are in delightful contrast to the familiar and hackneyed types that serve to represent Virtue, Sacrifice, Charity, and the other qualities which sculptors have personified, time out of mind, by large, heavy, dull-looking stone women. The sculpture throughout the Fair is of a character that deserves a more lasting form than it now possesses. A large proportion of the plaster figures of men, women, and animals which enrich the White City deserve to be preserved in bronze or marble infinitely more than most of the sculpture which is shown in the art gallery.

Hereafter the old charge that there is no art atmosphere in our country will, I think, prove a futile and groundless one. A single visit to the World's Fair must convince the most indifferent European-American that, whatever may have been the case at an earlier period, the country which has produced this great, harmonious, artistic whole is not entirely lacking in art atmosphere.

One of the pleasantest features of this building is the hospitality suggested throughout; the cool and quiet arcades where the visitor may sit and look out upon the varied scenes hourly enacted in that corner of the World's Fair; the roof-gardens, from which a fine view may be had of the distant buildings, with the shimmering lake beyond. Here one may dine comfortably and well, or enjoy "a dish of tea and talk," at the end of the long day of work and pleasure. Our building's highest mission perhaps will be to soothe, to rest, to refresh the great army of sight-seers who march daily through the Fair.

I have heard from these birds of passage various interesting comments on our building. One of these I remember as particularly expressive of its influence, coming as it did from a tired woman, who had labored generously and ceaselessly for many months at her little part of the great work. "I call it the flying building," she said; "it seems to lift the weight off my feet when I look at those big angels."

The interior decoration is as appropriate and simple as the exterior. Touches of gold, here and there, relieve the purity of the whitest building in all the White City. The Hall of Honor is unbroken by pillars or supports, and rises grandly to its seventy feet of height. It is 67½ feet wide and 200 feet long. Statistics, however, avail us but little in looking at this noble hall, and it is best to remember only that it is as high as our hopes for it have been. Honored names are here written in letters of gold—the names of women great in art, in song, in thought, in science, in statecraft, and in liter-

THE COLUMBIAN FOUNTAIN.

DESIGNED BY FREDERICK MACMONNIES.

COLUMBIA, ENTHRONED, IS PROPELLED BY THE ARTS AND SCIENCES AND STEERED BY FATHER TIME.

VIEW OF THE GREAT BASIN, LOOKING WEST.

Engraved by Rand, McNally & Co.

ature. Side by side with the sovereigns of Europe—Isabella, Elizabeth, and Victoria—are the names of the workers, the seers, the pioneers who long ago laid the true foundation of this building. Some of them are living still, thank God—women whose keen eyes

DECORATIVE PANEL—"ART, SCIENCE, AND LITERATURE."
LYDIA EMMET. UNITED STATES. (Copyrighted.)

foresaw the coming of the day that has dawned; the day of which John Stuart Mill said: "The women's hour has struck."

The north tympanum of the hall is enriched by a decorative painting by Mrs. Frederick MacMonnies, representing the Primitive Woman. At the other end Miss Mary Cassatt presents her

TAPESTRY. DESIGN ADAPTED FROM AN ANCIENT EMBROIDERY. BARBARA WOLF. GERMANY.

conception of Modern Woman. Mrs. MacMonnies' subject is well chosen and ably treated. On the extreme right we have a single male figure, a hunter clad in skins—he has just returned from the chase. A group of women and children bear away the game he has killed and minister to his wants. A kneeling girl crushes a bunch of grapes into a cup to refresh the tawny giant. In the middle grouping we have woman, the bearer of burdens, typified by a band of girls carrying water-jars. In the foreground a maiden bathes a laughing child in a clear stream, while a mother advances toward the water bearing two children in her arms. On the extreme left we see the sturdy daughters of the plow driving a yoke of milk-white oxen. A band of sowers scatters the grain in the new-made furrows, while one tired girl, kneeling in the fore-ground, drinks from a vase. The background of trees and water and distant land is excellently treated. The dark figures of two horsemen are to be seen at the extreme right. Mrs. MacMonnies' work is of a high order; it shows a true decorative sense, a sure hand, and a fresh, joyous imagination. Artistically and intellect-ually it is a composition which commends itself to all those who understand and honor the idea for which our building stands.

The central portion of Miss Cassatt's panel shows us a group of young women gathering apples in a pleasant orchard. On the right is a band of ladies variously engaged. One is playing upon a stringed instrument, while another poses in one of the attitudes of the modern skirt-dance. On the left we have Fame, a flying figure, pursued by a flock of ducks and women. The border of the tympanum is very charming; the children quite beautifully painted. Both Mrs. MacMonnies and Miss Cassatt received orders for their work from the Executive Board of the Woman's Building. The two decorations were executed in Paris and sent to Chicago.

Four large decorative panels enrich the sides of the hall.

New England's contribution to the decoration of the Woman's Building is shown in one of these large panels, which illustrates the duties and avocations of the Pilgrim Mothers and Daughters. The painter, Miss Lucia Fairchild of Boston, a young artist of great promise, has chosen for her subject a group of women engaged in domestic labor. In the foreground a kneeling girl is washing dishes in a pool of still water; one of her sisters stands beside her drying a pewter basin. On the left, under the porch of a humble cottage, a mother stands holding an infant in her arms. A girl sits by her spinning-wheel, whose threads have become entangled. One young matron holds a distaff, while a girl beside her is stitching

OIL PAINTING.—"ELAINE." FRAU VON PREUSCHEN. GERMANY.

on a white garment. At a little distance a group of children surround their teacher, who, with an open book upon her knees, is holding school out of doors. It is the springtime of the year and of the nation; from the green plain stretching toward the distant sea the trees lift their budding branches. In the background we have the traditional white meeting-house with its single spire, and over a newly broken road a pair of oxen draw a cart laden with wood; the man who drives them is necessarily a very small figure in this large, simple composition. The whole scene breathes the atmosphere of that early New England which has found its best interpreter in Hawthorne. The harsh but not inhospitable Plymouth coast, and the hardy settlers whose courage and resolution laid the foundations of the New England we know to-day, have been sketched by the young artist with a strong hand. The color scheme is cool and sober; the dress and bearing of the women reserved, simple, and full of character. The thought behind the picture needs no criticism, it is an assertion of the prime duties of woman, the home-maker and care-taker; it is a hint full of significance to our day and generation, reminding us that unless the higher education now open to our sex makes women better and wiser wives and mothers, it is a failure.

No stronger contrast to Miss Fairchild's decoration can be imagined than that presented by the neighboring panel, "Woman in Arcadia," by Amanda Brewster Sewell. The former represented a cool, demure springtime on the Plymouth coast. In Arcadia it is warm, luxurious summer. The color is rich and deep; the pair of half-nude girls in the foreground have a pagan loveliness; the distant group gathering oranges are fair as dream-women. Mrs. Sewell has found "the way to Arcady," and illustrates it to us very sympathetically. It seems quite fitting that in this great White City, this echo of Hellenic beauty, there should be an Arcadian corner, and it is not unsuitable that we should find this in the Woman's Building.

The pair of panels which are placed opposite to those just described are the work of those popular painters Rosina Emmet Sherwood and Lydia Emmet. Mrs. Sherwood's panel shows us the Republic welcoming her daughters and bestowing laurel crowns upon them. The composition of this panel is very good, and the architectural detail of the background is well studied. Miss Emmet's companion panel is strong in the same qualities as her sister's. Music, art, and literature are all personified in an exceedingly well-arranged group of female figures.

BLACK AND WHITE DRAWING—"ANON COMES APRIL IN HER JOLLITY."
ROSINA EMMET SHERWOOD. UNITED STATES. (From Harper's Magazine. Copyrighted.)

I shall now invite the reader to take a short stroll with me through the principal departments of our building. We will enter at the northern door, pass through the loggia, and find ourselves in the midst of the American exhibit of applied arts. Here all is so excellent that we can afford to lose nothing; every case deserves examination. As it is impossible to speak of all the beautiful work exhibited by associations and individuals, let us notice that of the " Associated Artists," the parent society from which so many schools of embroidery and design have sprung. The two directions in which this school expresses itself are in the weaving of textiles and tapestries. The textiles are among the most beautiful fabrics that have ever been woven; they are rich in color and exquisite in texture. Certain effects can be produced by the weaving of silk which no pigment can ever give, for the silk itself has a reflective quality which is found in no other medium. The tapestry from Raphael's cartoon of " The Miraculous Draught of Fishes " is a very remarkable work of art, and one which stands alone in modern needlework. The design was photographed from the painter's cartoon upon the linen, and the spirit of the original is very perfectly preserved.

The pottery comes next in interest to the textiles and embroideries. Nowhere is woman doing better work than in the manufacture and decoration of our native clays. We find original and beautiful vessels of use and ornament exhibited by many of the States. It is due to the Western States to say that in this branch of applied arts they surpass the Eastern.

However long we linger in this section of the building, we leave it with regret. The impression which we carry away from it is that we are no longer pensioners of Europe in the matter of designs. To-day we have an American School of Design, with a distinct national character of its own, and our women are to the fore in every one of its branches.

Passing through the corridor we enter the main hall, where there is much to admire in exhibitions of art and handicraft. The laces, in themselves, are a gallery of exquisite design and workmanship. There is no danger that the visitor will slight the Hall of Honor, so we will not linger here, but pass on to the southern pavilion. We have crossed the seas, Spain is before us; India, Germany, Austria, Belgium are upon our left; Sweden, Mexico, Italy, France upon the right. Two rooms of a Japanese house have been cunningly reproduced with the nicety and finish which characterize all the work of this artistic people. The low-ceiled boudoir is

4

CARTOON FOR STAINED GLASS. MARY E. McDOWELL. UNITED STATES.

carpeted with matting and hung with delicately tinted paper. In an outer room—a guest-chamber—is a raised cushion of state, on which the honored stranger is invited to sit (or squat). A few paintings hang upon the wall; a single piece of bronze, a finely modeled bird, rests on a lacquered stand. The inner room is sacred to the toilet of the lady of the house. Over a screen hang rainbow-hued garments enriched with wonderful embroideries. Lacquered coffers of every size and shape, tied with silk cords of different colors, form a picturesque substitute for our commonplace chests of drawers. A polished steel mirror, upon a stand, shows where the mistress of this dainty boudoir should sit upon a cushion to perform the details of her toilet. A lacquered and bronze brazier stands near, and a rack over which are folded fine linen towels. A multitude of fine inlaid boxes stand upon the ground near the mirror. Let us not pry into their secrets. The real secret of the peculiar charm which the Japanese women have always possessed for men of their own and the European nations lies in the fact that they are taught to be agreeable. With the Japanese, good manners rise to the dignity of a high art. Courtesy, gentleness, sympathy are cultivated with the same care and skill that this joyous, painstaking people put into everything that they do.

We must not fail to see the Japanese parlor in the second story, where the Japanese Commissioner has gathered together a very fine collection of painted and embroidered screens and hangings. A painting upon silk, framed in a little shrine in the end of this room, shows us Sei Shonagun, a learned Japanese woman who served the Empress Sada Ko in the tenth century of the Christian era. She wrote a book which is still famous, an extract from which we may read, in translation, together with a full description of the picture. Nothing brings home the real significance of the work collected in our building more than the statement made by the Japanese Woman's Commission of its organization. The report says: "Her Majesty the Empress of Japan, with her usual habits of helping any good work, especially for her own sex, most graciously pleased with the movement, generously bestowed a large gift to carry on the work of the commission. Princess Mori assumed the duty of chairman, and asked the members, who are mostly ladies of high rank, to act as committees. On the 13th of May, 1892, the first meeting of the commission was held at Shiba-Hama-Rikyn, a pleasure palace in Tokio. Since then, twice a month they have held regular meetings to consider the affairs of the commission."

The most important feature of the second story is the Assembly Hall, a large room lying on the north side of the building. It has a wide platform and is admirably adapted for meetings, lectures, and concerts. The three stained-glass windows which light the stage are all the work, and two of them the gifts, of Massachusetts women. The furniture, presented by the ladies' committee of Mobile, is simple and appropriate in design. A stained-glass window opposite the platform is the work and the gift of Pennsylvania women. It was in this room that the meeting was held on the 30th of April, when the commissioners from many of our own States and from some distant countries presented to Mrs. Palmer the gifts offered to the Woman's Building. Tokens and tidings of good-will from the four corners of the earth were generously offered and graciously accepted. The value of the gifts, the nationality of the givers, was forgotten in the deep significance of that meeting. Woman at last is rousing from her long sleep. We of the New World have called out for help, for sympathy. From the far Orient comes back an answer to our cry. The slave woman of the harem murmurs, "I hear!"

WATER-COLOR PORTRAIT.
ROSINA EMMET SHERWOOD. UNITED STATES.

The Assembly Hall and the Model Kitchen fill the whole of the northern end of the building. The space between the inner corridor and the outer arcade has been divided into eight admirably-shaped and well-lighted rooms. The Model American Kitchen gives an object lesson to housekeepers from all parts of the world.

Passing down the corridor to the right we find Connecticut's room, a bright, cheerful apartment, whose simple and appropriate decoration we owe to Miss Sheldon of Hartford.

We come next to the first of the two Record rooms, which on either side connect with the library. Here are kept the statistics of woman's work in many countries, which have been collected with such patient research. A frieze formed of panels of native wood, designed and carved by women from our different States, is an interesting feature of this room.

From a purely artistic standpoint the library is the most important feature of the building, after the Hall of Honor. Its decoration has been intrusted to Mrs. Wheeler. As the heavy doors swing to, we find ourselves in a well-proportioned room, whose chief and most valued quality is that of harmony. The eyes, tired with the great demand which has been made upon them, rest gratefully upon the green and gold of the walls. The visitor sinks into a chair, and for a long time thinks of nothing but the pleasant coolness of the place. The room has a character and individuality that we rarely find save in the house of some esthetic lover of books. The beautiful dark carved-oak book-cases are filled to overflowing with books by women of all nations. Every room has its own climate—we know whether we are visiting in the arctic, the temperate, or the torrid zone five minutes after entering a strange house. Our library is in the temperate zone—the best climate for the scholar and the dilettante. To such a visitor there is

SKETCH FOR GLASS WINDOW. MRS. PARRISH. UNITED STATES.

no single apartment in the whole Fair where he will find himself so pleasantly at home. The chief decoration of this room is the ceiling —the work of Dora Wheeler Keith. In undertaking this arduous labor Mrs. Keith attacked the most difficult branch of decoration, and the artist is to be congratulated that she has painted what is perhaps the rarest thing in the whole range of art, a successful ceiling.

The ornamentation is rich and original. A wide border of scroll-work forms the outer edge. Inside of this we have a very beautifully painted piece of drapery, enriched here and there with

CARTOON FOR MEMORIAL WINDOW.
HELEN MAITLAND ARMSTRONG. UNITED STATES.

bunches of lilies, which weaves itself into a sort of garland between the four medallions, each of which contains a symbolical figure. The oval wreath of lilies which encircles the central portion is a very beautiful and original feature of the decoration. The central group contains three figures. Science, a male figure, sits enthroned with Literature beside him, personified by a graceful woman; between the two stands Imagination, reconciling and binding Science and Literature to each other. The color scheme is cool, refreshing, and harmonious. In speaking of this admirable work, Mrs. Wheeler was heard to say: "I think it is a worthy composition." I have heard many more extravagant phrases applied to this decoration by connoisseurs and critics, but none has pleased me so much. It is indeed worthy of the honored name both mother and daughter bear—a name that is identified with such a potent influence for high taste, serious work, and honest endeavor. Among the founders of the new American school of design which has done so much for the education of our people, there is no figure more striking than that of Candace Wheeler.

Continuing our tour, we find ourselves in the room devoted to the exhibit of the English Training-School for Nurses. There is much that is valuable and interesting to study here; a wonderful basket trunk with compartments for caps and bandages, splints, bonnets, aprons, and all the other requisites for the personal comfort and professional duties of a soldier in the noble army of nurses. The room is graced with portraits of women whose names never fail to arouse an emotion when they are pronounced—Florence Nightingale, Sister Dora, and a score of other less famous sisters of humanity.

The Organization Room lies at the south end of the corridor. Here we may see the exhibit of over fifty associations of women. Opposite the library we have a suite of three rooms. The first of these, the Kentucky Parlor, is a very pleasant and cheerful room, with a flavor of the "old colonial" in its decoration and appointments.

We next pass into the Managers' Drawing-room, furnished, decorated, and maintained by the women of Cincinnati. It is a pleasant place to linger, and has many treasures of pottery and faience.

Beyond is the California Room, famous for its redwood. The ceiling, doors, and wainscoting are all made of this rich, mellow wood, the grain of which makes delicate lines and touches of light and color, which the high polish brings out finely.

SKETCH FOR WINDOW. MARY TILLINGHAST. UNITED STATES.

The education which the Woman's Building furnishes is not received through the eye alone; the ear comes into play for a very important share. Every morning, at 10 o'clock, an illustrated

PAINTED SCREEN. FRANCE.

lecture is given in the model kitchen by Mrs. Sarah Tyson Rorer. One of the special subjects treated by the teacher is the preparation of Indian corn. The kitchen, which is maintained at the expense

of the Illinois Ladies' Board, is really doing a missionary work.
Mrs. Rorer maintains that educated cooking is as much a science as
chemistry, and she thoroughly believes in the saying that "the
inventor of a new and wholesome dish is of greater value to his
fellow-creatures than the discoverer of a new planet." Of all the
pleasant features of our building, I have found nothing more interesting than these sessions with Mrs. Rorer. To hear the mysteries
of baking, roasting, and boiling intelligently explained, and to
watch at the same time the skillful preparation of a dainty dish, is a
pleasant and instructive occupation. The infinite variety of forms
into which the Indian corn can be transmuted by an intelligent
cook was a revelation to most of Mrs. Rorer's hearers.

Another pleasant educational exhibit of a similar nature is to
be found in the garden café, where Mrs. Riley, a graduate of the
Boston Cooking School, provides home cooking of the most appetiz-
ing description for the hungry sight-seer, but opens her kitchen for
public inspection every afternoon for an hour. The restaurant
serves a double purpose—it feeds the hungry visitor and educates
the inquiring mind of the housekeeper. The contrast between
this well-ordered establishment, where the dishes are properly
prepared and neatly served, and some of the other restaurants of
the Fair is very striking. Nowhere is the tired man or woman
so well treated and fed as in our model lunch-room.

The Committee of Congresses, of which Mrs. James P. Eagle is
chairman, has prepared a feast of reason, in which the public is
invited to participate. Either in the morning or the afternoon of
each day the Assembly Room in the Woman's Building will furnish
an amusement or lecture, which, like all the other matters connected
with our building, is given to the public gratis. Music has an
honored place in our temple. One afternoon of every week Mr.
Theodore Thomas and his well-trained orchestra give a concert of
popular classical music; it may be imagined that there is little room
to spare in the Assembly Hall on these occasions. Once in every
two weeks concerts are given by amateur musicians from different
parts of the country. The method pursued in securing the per-
formers is extremely good. The candidates first pass an examination in their own State, and then a second at Chicago before a
jury of experts appointed by Mr. Thomas. A diploma will be
awarded to the musicians who take part in these amateur concerts.
In this way the high standard of talent desired has been attained.
Women's musical clubs have been invited to participate, and,
thanks to the energy of Mrs. Francis B. Clarke, chairman of the

Committee of Music, and of Mrs. Thomas, who have had this branch of the work in charge, a musical congress has been arranged which promises to be one of the most interesting features of the Exposition.

Ceylon's contribution is most precious. She sends us not only the work of her people's hands but a band of her citizens. The Ceylon pavilion has two departments; one representing a temple, the other a resting-place near the temple. The beautifully carved pillars and arches of ebony are constantly surrounded by a group of admirers. The temple is adorned by a painting of Buddha and a marriage scene from a popular romance.

The hospitality of the Woman's Building! I must always come back to that. One day I was given, on entering, a fresh jasmine flower that had bloomed in Texas; a thousand were distributed that morning, thanks to the generosity of the women of Galveston. One afternoon when I crept into this haven, wearied from the feast of sight and sound, a slender, dusky-

EMBROIDERY. PUPILS OF THE HOUSE OF THE LEGION OF HONOR. FRANCE.

skinned Ceylonese offered me a cup of fragrant tea. The picturesque costumes, the refinement and grace of these silent servitors, their delicate hands and refined, intelligent faces make a deeper impression than the richest of the embroideries or the most artistic of the jewels shown in their pavilion. Man is more interesting than the noblest of his works. It is for their testimony of human skill, patience, and industry that we value the rare works of art and handicraft gathered in our building. Nowhere in the Exposition can we find so complete a history of the industries of the human race as in the Woman's Building; beginning with women's work in savagery (a very wonderful collection of which is to be seen in the Scientific Room) and ending with a modern woman's idea of that primitive woman as shown by Mrs. MacMonnies in her decoration. We thus see in one department the tools of the savage woman, and in another the representation of their use. Judging by her handicraft, the primitive woman worked earnestly and well. With here and there a few brilliant exceptions, the work of modern women in the higher fields of art has been less earnest, less thorough, than the work of these savage women. The religions of the Orient, which teach that man only is capable of civilization, and have made woman man's slave, are partly responsible for the long period of triviality in women's work. The savage woman is a dignified figure. On her falls the burden of weaving and basket-making, of sowing and reaping, of feeding and clothing her family. The legacy she has left us is infinitely precious and touching. Orientalism is responsible for the idea that woman is the inferior of man, and when I hear women lightly professing a belief in Buddhism, I always feel like reminding them that one of the fundamental ideas of that religion is that the female principle in the universe is the principle of evil. To-day Christianity has only just begun, after nineteen hundred years, to overcome this paralyzing idea of the inferiority of our sex. Fifteen years ago, nay ten years ago, I might almost say five, the women artists of Europe and of America, while showing a great deal of talent, betrayed a lack of power, conscience, and persistence in their work. It had the qualities of imagination, of sweetness, of romance, and of color, but it lacked the sterner qualities of technique which only the severest study, the most scrupulous patience, the quality which I can perhaps best designate as the artistic conscience, can give. The

SKETCH FOR WINDOW.
MRS. J. B. WESTON. UNITED
STATES.

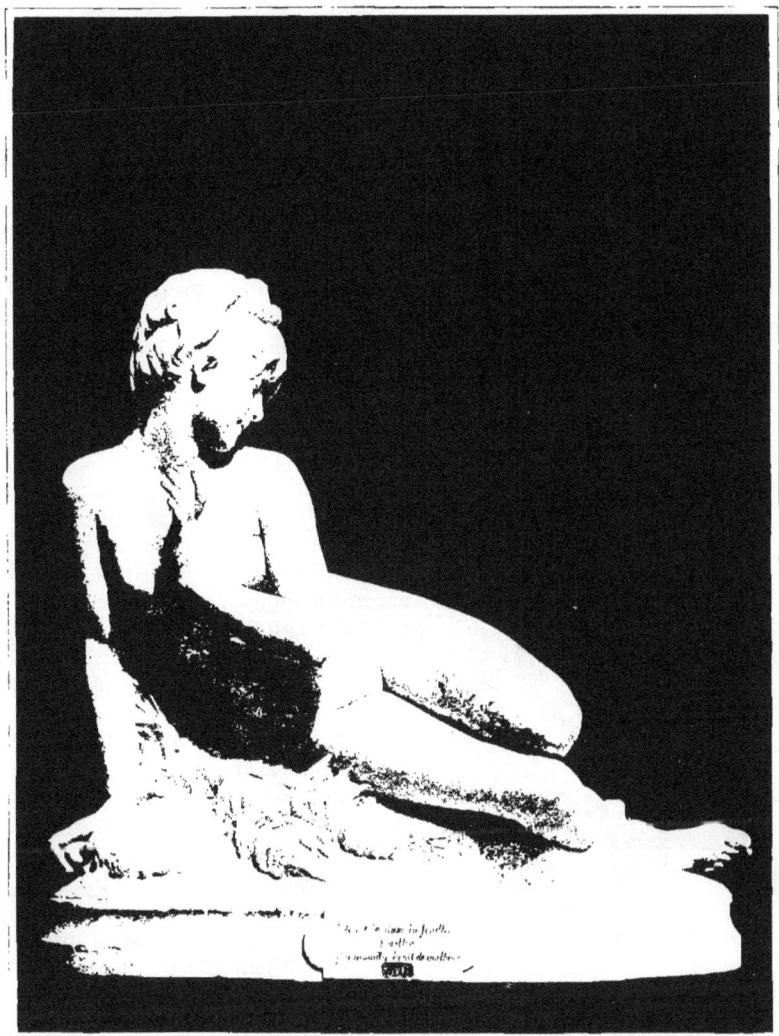

YOUNG GIRL BATHING. MME. LÉON BERTAUX. FRANCE.

old idea that woman's work in the higher fields is something phenomenal obtained both with the critics and with the women workers themselves. To-day the struggle for bread has become so fierce that no allowance is made for sex. We are at the dawn of a new era, when woman's labor shall be judged by the same inflexible standard of excellence as man's. Surely we may be excused if we have shown a little too much enthusiasm on this subject, for the gain is an immense one, not to woman alone, but to the whole race. There is no gain without a corresponding loss. There is no advance in which something is not left behind. In our country

WATER-COLOR PORTRAIT.
Rosina Emmet Sherwood.
United States. (Copyrighted.)

woman has always been a privileged person; and while we hold that rights are higher than privileges, it can not be denied that it is a little trying to see those privileges steadily diminishing; but it has now become a question of necessity, not of choice. The results of our public-school system are shown in the enormous number of men who are fitted for both the higher and lower branches of intellectual labor. A few months ago a gentleman in New York advertised in the same paper for a secretary and a butler. Five hundred applicants appeared for the secretaryship and two for the place of the butler. Competition in brain labor is so fierce, the price it secures so small, that to-day a large proportion of our artists, architects, literary and professional men find it impossible to support their families in the position to which their education entitles them. Every year it is becoming more expensive to live the life of cultivated people. The price of bread and meat and coal may be reduced as the demand for these articles increases, but the price of the luxuries and the graces of life increases in an exact ratio with the increase of population. A professional man, the son of a professional man, is too often faced with this problem: "How can I give my children as good an education as I myself received, when my income is only as large as my father's was and the expenses of education have doubled?" The wife, the sister, or the daughter is called in council. It is quite evident to her that the man can not support his wife and his children as they should be supported, and the family must either take a lower position in the social scale, or, as the only other alternative, the women must contribute to the expenses of the household. It is this economic necessity which has forced the vast army of women workers into the higher fields of labor.

Now that we have wandered through the pleasant arcades, the quiet library, the busy, energetic Hall of Honor, let us leave the Woman's Building and the "White City," go down to the shore of the lake, look out over its changeful waters, and think. What does it all amount to? Palaces of marble and brick crumble away and leave no sign to show where they have stood, and this mock-marble city is as evanescent as a dream. With that curious commercial sense which is perhaps our most salient national characteristic, many hundreds of people have asked the same question: "Does it pay?" Of no department in the whole Exposition has there been so much doubt expressed on this point as of the Woman's Building. It has had its enemies from the very hour of its inception; honest and

"THE WOOD DOVE."
MARY HALLOCK FOOTE. UNITED STATES.
(By permission of the Century Company—
Copyrighted.)

dishonest enemies. It is only the former with which we must concern ourselves. These have pointed out the very great outlay of time, strength, and money which have gone to make up the harmonious whole; they have pointed out that a great number of the best women workers have elected to exhibit the fruits of their labor side by side with that of their brothers. These critics ask: "Is it not unfair to show as women's work what is only a partial representation of it?" The answer to this objection lies in the fact that the building is among the most interesting features of the Fair. It has never undertaken to show all, or half, that woman is doing. Such an exhibit would be impossible, even were it housed in so vast a structure as the Palace of the Liberal Arts. From the first, the idea has been held by those in authority that the building's mission

SKETCH FOR WINDOW.
L. F. EMMET, UNITED STATES. (Copyrighted.)

was more moral than material. It was designed to represent chiefly that part of woman's labor which finds no place in the other departments of the Fair. Perhaps the most valuable thing it has accomplished is the bringing together of women from the most distant parts of the world. Who can foretell how potent an influence for the unity of the nations may spring from this meeting of the Slav and the Teuton, the Celt and the Mongol, the Gaul and the Latin, the Greek and the Anglo-Saxon? From the days of Helen, women have been accounted a cause for strife between men and nations. *"Cherchez la femme"* is the old saying whenever there is trouble afoot. If this is true, nothing can be so important for the peace of the world as that these prime causes of difference among men should become friends and allies. If the three goddesses had handed back the apple to Paris and said " Thank you," a mighty pother of arms might have been saved and the greatest poem in the world lost. In our modern contest, each participant strives not to take from but to give to her sisters the palm. In many of the other departments of the Fair there has been an infinite amount of political friction. One country will not exhibit because our duties are unjust, another will put itself to very little trouble for us because it has so little commercial relation with our own. We find nothing of this in the Woman's Building. We find a singleness of purpose which is truly impressive. The queens of England, of Spain, and of Italy take part in our enterprise; the empresses of Japan and of Russia testify their interest; the wife of the president of the French Republic lends us her countenance, and the great ladies of Germany, Belgium, Sweden, Norway, Denmark, Russia, Austria, and all the other nations represented in our building have put their hands to our work.

The Queen of England, her daughters, and her granddaughters send us their handiwork. Not only have the great ladies lent us their countenance, but the work-women all over the world have helped to enrich our building. In the Spanish section we notice the neatly rolled cigarettes of the cigarette-makers and the nets of the fisher-wives lying near the rich embroideries of the nuns, the exquisite missals from the convent schools, the paintings and writings of royal amateurs. The insane women of a Pennsylvania almshouse make a contribution of neatly embroidered linen to our applied arts. The little children of the charity schools of Paris send us drawings and maps of so exquisite a workmanship that it is difficult to realize that the signatures, " Rachel, aged 13," and "Helene, aged 14," belong to their authors.

Many lessons may be learned at the World's Fair, and many in the Woman's Building; the most important of these is the unity of human interests. No man or woman who has truly entered into the life of the White City, which is not Chicago's, nor the United States', nor the Americas', but the world's city, can ever again be satisfied with mere city or State citizenship. In this miniature world we have tasted world's citizenship, we have learned that nothing that is not for the good of humanity at large can benefit us or our country.

MAUD HOWE ELLIOTT.

5

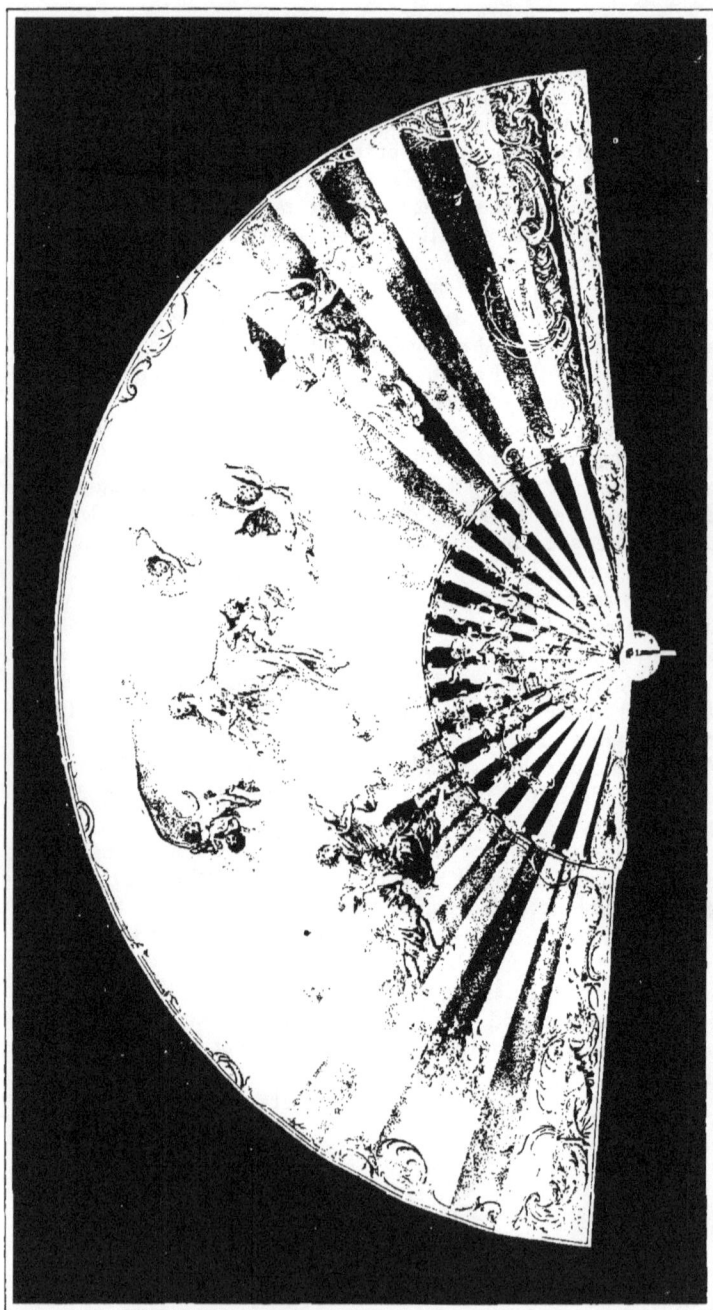

FAN—"AURORA." EXHIBITED BY THE MAISON AHRWEILER. FRANCE.

WOMAN IN ART.

NOT unreasonable and as capable of proof as any other legend about the matter is this, that the first artist was not he who "stayed by the tents with the women;" neither Cleanthes, nor Telephanes, but rather was it some happy mother, dreaming dreams by a river, watching the shadows of leaves and flowers come and go, making garments for her man-child, her desire being to her lord. And the shadows of the leaves and flowers fell upon the garments, and then the artist-soul was born, and designed quaint patterns from them to beautify the robe. Penelope drew her own designs upon the shroud she broidered for old Laërtes, and the naïve drawing of the Bayeux tapestry was from Queen Mathilde's unaccustomed hand, for the men had gone forth to do battle.

Ariosto's much-quoted lines, "Women have risen to high excellence in every art whereto they give their care," is proven in a long line of illustrious women who have been artists, beginning with Helena, daughter of Timon of Egypt, and continuing to our own Mary Cassatt.

From the beginning there have always been those who have stepped from out the ranks of women and stood beside the men.

It is no new thing that they should teach, or paint, or write; and if as yet in art there are none who are equal with the masters, they stand immediately behind, unafraid, biding their time, for "art happens," and one day Apollo will find one of our own sex to smile upon, and these will walk with the chosen one, who will be of the few who live for all time.

It is the fashion to deny women originality. Art is but an imitation, and among the great men of our time, who are they whose inspiration is far to seek? It is a long time ago since the wisest man said:

> "There is nothing new under the sun."

Among the ancients, Pliny mentions many women painters who were famous.

Helena, daughter of Timon of Egypt, was living in the year

400 B. C. Of her only recorded work, "The Battle of Issus," there is a mosaic reproduction at Naples.

Anaxandra, daughter of Nealces of Cicyon, lived in Egypt, 200 B. C.

Aristarette was the daughter and pupil of Nearchus. She was famed for her portrait of Esculapius.

Of the women of our own era, the earliest of whom we have knowledge is Margareta Van Eyck, born in 1370, sister and fellow-worker of the master Van Eyck; and somewhere it is written how she helped to perfect the method of painting with oils. Of her work there is here and there in the world somewhat for the curious expert to discover. In the National Gallery of London we may see a Madonna and Child by Margareta, and, most interesting of all, the famous Bedford Missal, now in the Bibliotheque Nationale at Paris.

Among the women of the fifteenth, sixteenth, and seventeenth centuries, we have Saint Catherine of Bologna, the beauty of whose life was equaled by the beauty of her missal painting, and Maria de Abarca, a distinguished portrait painter, even at a time when the Master of Madrid raised Spanish art to its highest.

Sophonisba Angosciolo of Cremona was another celebrated portrait and *genre* painter. She was invited to Spain by Philip II., the great art patron of his time. She painted the portrait of Queen Isabella to the entire satisfaction of Pius IV., to whom the king presented it. Her pictures are to be found in many collections, and her portraits of herself show her to have been both beautiful and clever.

Mention should be made of Artemisia Gentileschi, Catherine Ginassi, Paladini, Teodora Danti, Coriolano, Veronica Fontana, Suor Plantilla Nelli (whom Vasari extols), Diana Ghisi, Isabella Parasole, Agnese Dolci (daughter of Carlo Dolci), and Elizabetta Sirani, whose beautiful Madonna and Child is one of the treasures of the gallery at Bologna.

Looking from the south to the north, we find Sabina Stienbach. What a proud moment it must have been for her when the master Dürer purchased from her a *plattlcin illuminirt, cin salvator—* "which was a wonder."

Maria Merian was also a German. Her miniatures have seldom been equaled for beauty and delicacy of color. In the British Museum are two volumes containing her drawings of insects and plants, which were purchased by Sir Hans Sloane for five guineas a drawing.

STATUE OF COLUMBUS AT THE EASTERN ENTRANCE OF THE ADMINISTRATION BUILDING.
JOINT WORK OF MISS MARY T. LAWRENCE AND MR. ST. GAUDENS.

AGRICULTURAL BUILDING.

Engraved by Rand, McNally & Co.

Size, 800 x 500 feet.   Architects, Messrs. McKim, Meade & White.   Cost, $618,000.

Then there was Anne Killegrew, of whom Dryden wrote she—

* * "perfectly could represent
The shape, the face with every lineament."

She was also—

"A grace for beauty, a muse for wit."

Caroline Watson's engravings are very fine, and compare favorably with her contemporary, Bartolozzi's.

Madam Vigée-Lebrun's portraits are all charming, some of them great, and, as some one has recently said, "preserve to us the thoughts and aspirations of the women of 1775-1789."

Angelica Kauffman—Miss Angel, as the English called her—is familiar to all the world. Every honor that it was possible to

SUGGESTION FOR REREDOS. MRS. KENYON COX. UNITED STATES.

bestow upon an artist was hers. From praising her work too much the world has come to praising it too little, but it is certain that for her time her pictures were remarkable. Her etchings are considered very fine, and are much sought after.

It is impossible in so little space to tell of all the famous women painters and their achievements—women whose works are precious to the *cognoscenti*, if not household words to "the one who wanders about."

One of the many interesting exhibits in the Woman's Building is a comprehensive collection of etchings and engravings. It includes examples of the earliest work of women in this field, beginning with that of Marie di Médicis and Diana Ghisi, and ending with the admirable productions of Caroline Watson, Mary Cassatt, Louise Abbema, Mrs. Moran, Mrs. Getcher, and Mme. Bracquemond.

Women painters have always excelled in portraiture, certainly the most difficult, if not the highest, branch of art. It is an odd thing too that art finds its best expression now in the north, among the women as among the men. To go as far north as possible, the number of Swedish and Norwegian women who have won honors in France far outranks that of any other nation.

No matter how much one claims for the women who have lived, for the women who now live one can claim more. Rosa Bonheur has painted pictures which entitle her to the high position which she occupies. Marie Cazin, in both sculpture and painting, has achieved high distinction. Virginie Demont-Breton is hardly less distinguished in art than her illustrious father. A German, Dora Hitz, is found worthy to be a member of the fastidious "Champ-de-Mars," while Alix d'Anéthan, a Belgian, is also a member of this exacting society. Some of the best work in the last exhibition of this same *Société Nationale* was contributed by Marie Breslau, a Swiss, a member of the society from the time of its organization in 1890.

PORTRAIT SKETCH.
ALLEGRA EGGLESTONE. UNITED STATES.

A famous Danish woman is Anna Archer. Emma Lowstadt Chadwick is a Swede whom we wish we might claim, since she is the wife of an American. Anna Bilinska is a Pole.*

In England there are many women painters who rank quite above the average Englishman. Mrs. Stanhope Forbes, whom we would also like to claim, since she began her art career in the schools of the New York Art League, paints more beautiful pict-

*An interesting picture by that remarkable young Russian, Marie Bashkirtseff, may be seen among the French pictures in the Woman's Building.—[ED.]

ures than those of her very talented husband, while technically
her work is as good as his.

But we would give most praise to the work of our own women,
for to their Anglo-Saxon temperament they add a Gaelic ability.

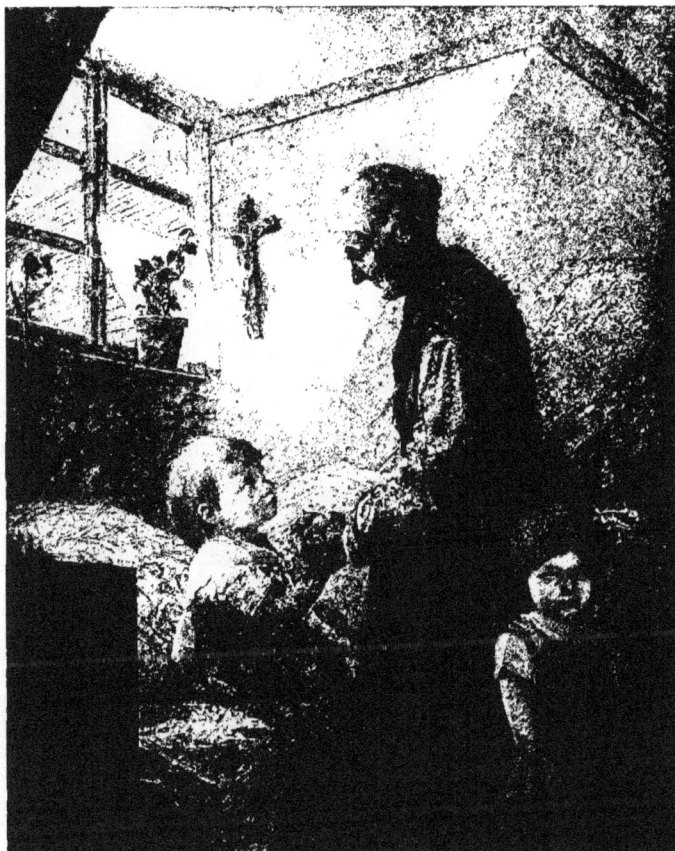

OIL PAINTING—"MORNING PRAYER." C. E. FISCHER. GERMANY.

To-day the American woman enters every art and every industry,
and enters it successfully.

Some time ago a master of the Art Students' League of New
York, on being questioned as to whether women students did good
work, said the average of excellence among the women was much

higher than among the men; that he was continually being surprised by their perseverance and originality. This might mean
little, since woman is quicker to "arrive," but it shows that at any
rate her spirit is modern and diligent.

In France the first women to enter a life-class with men were
two Americans, and at the time, though it caused much talk, they
were admired for it. They held that if they were to compete with

OIL PAINTING—"MARS AND VENUS." POPPE LÜDERITZ. GERMANY.

men, they must have the same advantages; they must work with
them, be subject to their criticism, treated as comrades; and they
were. They held their own and wore "unspotted raiment."

Two women have been chosen to paint each a very important
decoration for the Woman's Building at Chicago—Miss Cassatt and
Mrs. MacMonnies. Miss Cassatt is easily the best of our women

painters. Her work is probably better known to those intimately connected with art than to the general public. She is of the school of Degas, Whistler, and Monet, and holds that a ballet-girl by Degas may be as religious as a saint by Puvis de Chavannes. She would call Degas master, but that her manner of expression has been arrived at independentiy of him. A set of her etchings has been purchased for the Luxembourg, and the French Government invited her to present it with a picture, an honor which falls to few, and which it was characteristic of Miss Cassatt to decline. Her "Essais Japonais" are what their title indicates, and are a revelation of strong line and exquisite

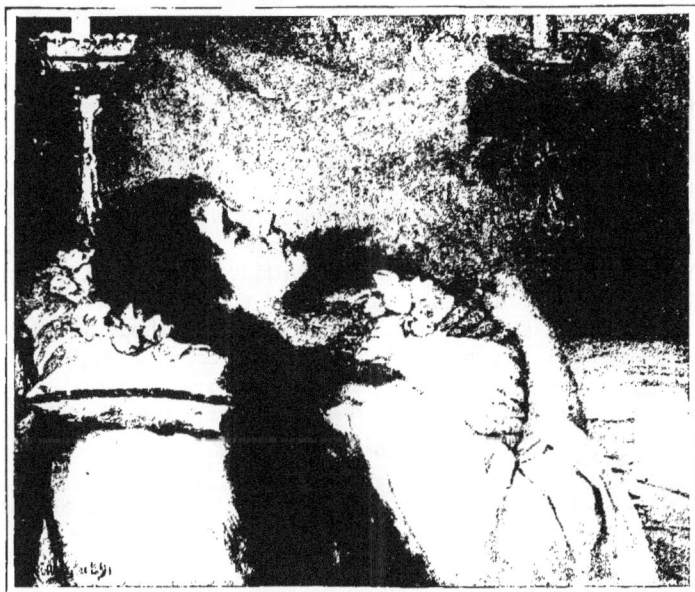

OIL PAINTING—"DEATH OF MIGNON." ADRIENNE POTTING. AUSTRIA.

color. Her decoration in Chicago will no doubt be *caviar* to those who may not see the religion in Degas, but to the catholic lover of art it appeals strongly.

Mrs. MacMonnies is a painter with a delightful color sense. It might seem rash that so young a painter should have been given, and that she should undertake, so grave a work. The decoration, which is sixty feet long, has been carried to a successful completion, and proves that the commendation she received from such men as Puvis de Chavannes and Cazin was not undeserved.

The only picture by a woman ever purchased by the trustees of the Chantry Bequest Fund for the South Kensington Museum was painted by an American, Mrs. Anna Lea Merritt, and it may be interesting to know that the oil and water-color copies of Turner's pictures given to the students of the South Kensington schools to copy from are by May Alcott Nierken, an American who died in 1879. *

At the last annual exhibition of the Water Color Society in New York a woman, Sara C. Sears, was given, for the first time, the prize for the best picture. The justness of the award was apparent to all.

To a woman *should* have been given, if justice were unalterable, not only the prize for the best picture by a woman, but also the prize for the best picture, irrespective of sex, seen at the recent exhibition of the New York Academy.

In the short space allotted to woman in art, it is impossible to mention even a few of the best of our women artists without seeming invidious, there are among us so many women artists whose work is serious and fine. We prefer that they should speak for themselves, as surely they have an opportunity of doing in Chicago.

To that critic who is to come, when the dragon of bad art ("which is the Devil and Satan") is bound for a thousand years, "and a seal is set upon him that he should deceive the nations no more," and the millennium of great American art is come, we commend our women artists, for no small part will they contribute; and we hope the dawn of that great day will be in Chicago.

S. T. HALLOWELL.

* Mrs. Nierken was the sister of Louisa Alcott, and the original of the character of Beth in " Little Women."

THE WESTERN FAÇADE OF THE ELECTRICITY BUILDING,

LOOKING TOWARD THE NORTH.

THE MARINE CAFÉ, WITH THE BRAZILIAN BUILDING IN THE BACKGROUND TOWARD THE LEFT.

APPLIED ARTS IN THE WOMAN'S BUILDING.

A NOTICE of the Applied Arts in the Woman's Building must begin with the specimens of antique art which belong to the collections of different countries in what is called the Foreign Section—exhibits which comprise the arts of embroidery, fan-painting, jewelry, silverware, and the exclusively feminine art of lace-making.

The collection of Queen Margherita covers not only the long history of the lace-making art of Italy, but that of all lace-making countries as well, while in other foreign exhibits are found ecclesiastical and antique embroideries of all nations, treasures of all countries, centuries, epochs, and schools. Not gleanings, but selections from the precious arts of all countries are here, since among these it is always the most valuable, the costliest, the most difficult of accomplishment, which receives the care of succeeding generations, and survives for the inspiration, guidance, and standard of mankind. It is wonderful that such treasures, under even the most careful convoyance, should have floated down the centuries and been allowed to drift to a country so far removed and undreamed of when some of them were created.

But it is not alone from foreign countries that these riches are gathered. An American collection, owned and loaned by citizens of New York, and collected by the New York State Board of Women Managers, is shown in the west gallery of the Rotunda. It does not by any means represent the wealth of curios and works of art possessed in this country, or even in New York City alone, but enough is shown to illustrate the very best periods of creative art, and to prove that if these private treasures could be occasionally gathered into public exhibitions, students and artists need not cross the great barrier of the sea to study examples of ancient knowledge and skill.

In passing from the best work of the past to that of to-day, and especially to that which is exclusively the work of the women of to-day, we must remember that, as far as practice is concerned, we are considering a new birth, a revival of ancient handcrafts, instead

WALL PANEL. ROYAL SCHOOL OF ART EMBROIDERY, VIENNA. AUSTRIA.

of a continuous exercise of them; and not only a revival, but an adaptation of them to new circumstances. Some of these arts had been practically dead for a hundred years. This consideration, while accounting for less exact execution, adds interest to the subject in showing the greater breadth given to every form of art by the modern diffusion of wealth, and possible gratification of taste in the individual. While the variety of direction is narrowed by the exhibits being exclusively the work of women, enough in all lines is shown to cause surprise even in this particular; since few are aware how much artistic labor is performed by women in the new directions of designing, cutting, leading, and painting of stained glass, of designs for book-making, both covers and illustrations; of designs for textiles and wall-hangings, drawing and modeling for silver-work, and in many other directions absolutely new to women. This is seen not only in the American Section, but in those of England, France, and Germany.

Those who believe in the application of the broadest and most thorough art-knowledge to mechanical processes have looked forward with apprehension to a collection of the work of women offered for competition and for the inspection of an art-loving world.

The exhibits of the Woman's Building are, however, entirely reassuring, and go to show, not only that art is a heritage common to both man and woman, but that both general and particular study have gone to the accomplishment of fine results. In examples of stained glass it is especially noticeable that simplicity and strength characterize the exhibits, and that the necessities and advantages of the art are well understood. Very few of the examples suggest the amateur gloss of the woman painter; in fact the most of it shows the result of careful study in a special direction, and an intention of mastery of the art as a profession. Certainly no one looking at some of these beautiful examples would characterize them as effeminate or weak. They are shown in a pavilion in the American Section, as well as in the Assembly Room, the California Room, and the Record rooms.

The embroidery exhibited by the Societies of Decorative Art and the Exchanges from many of our cities is of so high an order, that even those most familiar with the subject can hardly fail to be surprised with the very large amount of first-rate work exposed. There is no single specimen of embroidery which proves more conclusively that needlework is a form of artistic expression than the very remarkable piece of ecclesiastical embroidery, from that wonderful design of William Blake's, illustrating the lines: " When

6

the morning stars sang together, and all the sons of God shouted for joy." The design was photographed directly from the etching upon the linen, the entire surface of which is covered with Kensington stitchery of the most curious blending. The picture is one of Blake's most beautiful creations. The four figures with raised arms, typifying the stars, are partially clad in a drapery which seems to grow from the body as a garment of flesh. This curious idea is rendered even more fully apparent in the embroidery than in the original etching, as the color helps to produce this very original effect. The devotional spirit of the artist has been perfectly preserved, and it is not too much to say that this piece of needlework has an inspirational quality.

EMBROIDERED LANDSCAPE—"APPLE BLOSSOM TIME." A. J. PETERS. UNITED STATES.

The beginning of the modern American school of needlework dates from the exhibit of the Kensington school at our Centennial, seventeen years ago. Before that time, it can not be said to have had a truly national existence. To-day the American school stands foremost in originality of design, and in breadth of thought and method. Certain processes which belong to the oldest oriental embroidery, such as a combination of applique and embroidery, which were ignored by the English school as being irregular, have been adopted by individuals among us, and have produced most wonderfully artistic results. A noticeable feature of the American school is that its followers seize upon every means of expression, and use the common domestic darning stitch, or any

REPRODUCTION OF A LOUIS XV. WINDOW.
EXECUTED FOR PRESIDENT CARNOT. EMBROIDERED BY MLLE. BERTHE FLOURY, MLLE.
EUGENIE FRITMAN, MME. DUBOR. FRANCE.

other needlework stitch, to produce a desired effect; very much as
a sculptor may pick up and use any bit of wood, or his own thumb,
as a modeling tool, rather than the neatly turned instruments of
his trade.

The color sense which distinguishes our people is found as
much in the embroiderers as with the painters. Both the English
and our own embroiderers surpass the European and the orientals in
this respect. As far as pure technique goes, the Turkish Com-
passionate Fund shows the best work exhibited. The workers
have the advantage of
the inherited skill,
which surpasses all
other, and are directed
in the use of color by
English taste. Sweden
sends us some fine ex-
amples, and France
shows admirable work,
but it is among our own
women that we find the
highest grade of em-
broidery. The produc-
tions of the Americans
are scholarly, but not
academic. They are
full of fresh originality,
and the motto of our
needlewomen seems to
be that they must use
the rules that have here-
tofore governed their art, but that they must not be hampered
by them in their own fresh, spontaneous growth.

DESIGN FOR CARPET.
LUCY W. VALENTINE. UNITED STATES.

In the great American revival of stained glass, our women are
doing much creditable work. Many of the best firms, including
that of Tiffany, employ women designers, who have met with very
great success. Fifteen years ago, no American manufacturer
thought of buying an American design for his carpet, or wall-
paper, or textile. The usual thing to do was to buy a yard of
French or English material, and reproduce its color and design.
To-day the manufacturers all agree that the most popular designs
they can furnish are made by our native designers, who are, to a
very large extent, women. In the exhibit of the Pratt Institute,

very fine work in the designs of wall-paper and silk may be seen. Several of these have won prizes. This exhibit is well worth studying, for, while this institute is in its first year, many of its students are among our most skillful young designers.

In the exhibits of the various American ceramic clubs, societies, and leagues, the excellence of technique, as well as the variety and amount of work in this branch of art, is a genuine surprise. It is very rich in porcelains, following Sèvre and Dresden styles, but curiously lacking in the dash and freedom of modern French china painting. This seems to indicate that painters possessing force and originality find more congenial directions for their efforts. Exact skill, fineness of execution, and clever specimens of miniature art are far in excess of instances of color effect or original design, and there is as yet no foreshadowing of a distinctively American school of china decoration. This is the more remarkable in the face of

DESIGN FOR WALL PAPER.
ANNA LEE, UNITED STATES.

the evident popularity of the art, and the wide extent of its practice.

There are exquisitely painted specimens which come from places remote from centers of art, places where the student and artist must depend for educational influences entirely upon books or art publications. This undoubtedly retards the development

resulting from emulation, while it fosters the excellencies of technique.

American china decoration is not as wide in its scope as either the modern French or English schools, and certainly has not given us what we have a right to expect from so much and such excellent practice, namely, a development of design and method which shall be as characteristic of American thought as is shown in manufacture of silver and other metals, in embroideries, in illustration of literature, in design for textiles and wall-hangings, and in other

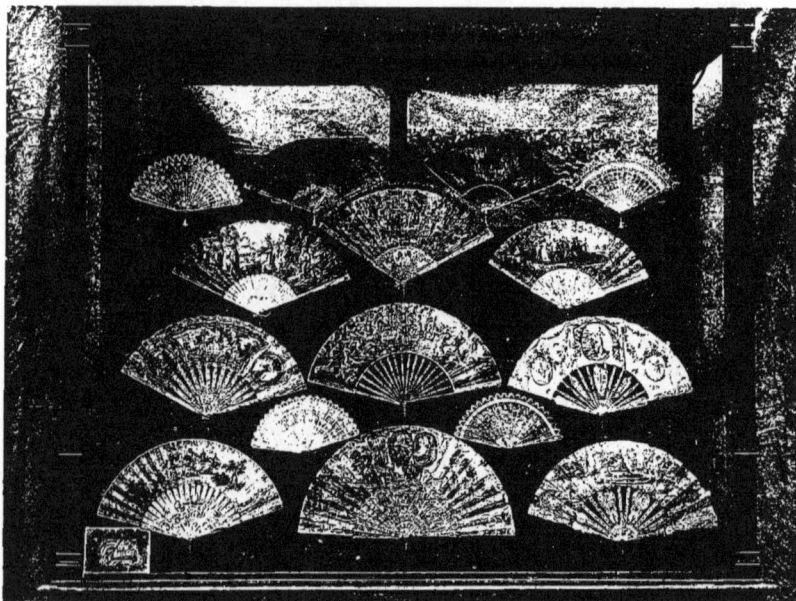

FANS. EXHIBITED BY E. BUISSOT. FRANCE.

directions of applied art. The one original development is that of the Rookwood pottery, exquisite specimens of which are to be seen in the Cincinnati Room. The glazes and colors, the lustrousness, the almost iridescent shadings place this ware very high in the history of modern production.

In book-covers and illustrations the largest number belongs to the exhibit of the applied arts of New York, Boston, and Philadelphia. It is noticeable and delightful that some of the book-covers exhibited are not merely copies or imitations of those of any style or period preëminent in the art of book-binding, but, while showing a wide knowledge of previous accomplishments in this line, and a familiarity with the old masters of the art, there is often a clever reference to the subject-matter of the book in the decorative treatment of the cover. For instance, the attractive outside of a book called "A Girl's Life Eighty Years Ago" shows the design and method of a sampler of the same period, lettering and borders appearing in the small block-work of the cross-stitch in the red and black sewing-silks peculiar to sampler work.

There are many others which illustrate very clearly the point that thought should be given not only to the *art* of the cover, but to its connection with the book itself, and indicate that the library of modern books will soon be more interesting from the outside than even the most classic use of leather and tooling could make it. An appropriate cover is like an open door into a pleasant interior, or like the skin of fruit which indicates its kind, as the color of the orange invites one to the flavor of the orange.

But while book-covers are so interesting from a book-lover's point of view,

DRAGON PLATE.
PARSONS & BROWN. UNITED STATES.

the large collection of book illustrations appeal to book-lovers and lovers of all good art. Many prominent publishers have contributed to this collection, and illustrations are shown in black and white, in water-colors, and in pen-drawings for many recent publications.

There is enough here to show more than the average excellence of the art of illustration as it stands to-day, not only in America but in all countries. There is no one great work which is like a monument placed at the highest point the art has reached, but there are many single pictures which are delightful, showing not only power of characterization and expression of sentiment, but admirable composition and draughtsmanship.

CANDACE WHEELER.

WATER-COLOR — DECORATIVE PANEL. MADELAINE LEMAIRE. FRANCE.

WOMEN ILLUSTRATORS.

CONTRASTING the Columbian Exposition witn our Centennial, the thoughtful observer is impressed with the great advance in art sentiment, in all phases of its expression, since that time.

Women have not been left behind in the march of events, and that their advance along the lines of progress and culture has been phenomenal is the only conclusion that can be arrived at after studying the subject. If this be true, speaking generally —and the most casual observer will hardly deny the statement—it is particularly pertinent in regard to their hold on art.

"THE LETTER OF RESIGNATION."
MARY HALLOCK FOOTE, UNITED STATES.
By permission of the Century Co.
(Copyrighted.)

There is no branch of art that shows more conclusively the higher standards demanded from its devotees among all classes of people than illustration. About twenty years ago, we could count on the fingers of one hand all the women seriously engaged in this work; nor was it until the advent of Mrs. Mary Hallock Foote in the field, as the illustrator of her own charming stories, that illustration seemed to present an opening for women. Having obtained an entering wedge, they were not long in availing themselves of their opportunity, and now it is an acknowledged fact that any woman possessing the requisite talent, training, and practical experience in working for reproduction, is assured a profitable return for her labor. The feminine mind has ceased to view a professional career as a thing of a few years only, a mere incident in her life to bridge over some financial crisis, or gratify a whim; nor is she following art in a dilettante spirit. She enters our schools and studies with a determination to learn all she possibly can from steady, grinding, academic work, and from her teachers. To this end she spends years in the up-hill, uninteresting pursuit of training the eye to a sense of proportion and construction before she attempts really serious work. She has learned to "wait with all her might."

If there is one characteristic beyond another that the average American woman possesses, it is an "instinct for expansion." She has an unquenchable thirst for information, a love of knowledge for its own sake; this actuating impulse has resulted in her development in all directions. If we consider Mrs. Foote the pioneer as an artist illustrator, it seems incredible that, considering the comparatively few years her drawings have been before the public, there should be so many illustrators to dispute the field with her. Let us take, for instance, Dora Wheeler Keith, whose figure-work shows a grace of line and sense of balance indicating a strong decorative tendency, and an insight into the realm of fanciful creation. Rosina E. Sherwood's illustrating possesses solid qualities and evidences of versatility in handling and subject, her drawings ranging from purely imaginative creations to the delineation of ultra-fashionable life. Rhoda Holmes Nicholls stands at the very head and front as a painter in water-colors, and is the recipient of medals both here and abroad. Though an English

DESIGNS FOR BOOK COVERS. ALICE C. MORSE (by permission of Messrs. G. P. Putnam & Sons). UNITED STATES.

woman by birth and training, she has found in America her greatest success. A strong sense of the picturesque, good draughtsmanship, and an unerring handling of her medium, characterize her illustrative work.

ILLUSTRATED PAGE FROM NURSERY RECEIPTS.
MARY HATHAWAY NYE. UNITED STATES.

Philadelphia is justly proud of Alice Barber Stephens. She has marked ability, a general all-round capacity for grasping the salient point in a story, and illustrating it sympathetically.

The pen-drawings of Allegra Eggleston are well "understood;" they show careful training and individuality of style. Her portrait work with the pen is particularly clever.

Lydia Field Emmet is in her happiest vein in depicting children. She is so successful here that one would almost wish she would confine herself exclusively to this field.

There is a constantly growing demand for good illustrators who can give a natural, sympathetic rendering of child-life. Miss Emmet is not, however, by any means alone in the arena. Among the contributors to children's periodicals are Miss Hills, equally sure in strong, bold outline and extremely delicate pen and ink work; Miss Kobbé, with her clever character sketches; Katherine Pyle, recognized by a certain quaint originality, and Miss Minna Brown; in fact nearly all the women illustrators work more or less for children's magazines.

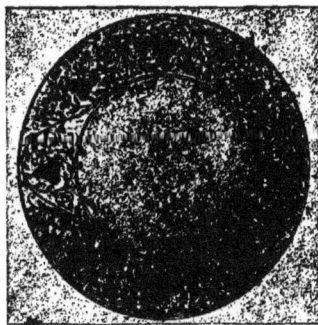

DESIGN FOR BOOK COVER.
MARY HATHAWAY NYE. UNITED STATES.

We regret the withdrawal of Maria Oakey Dewing from magazine work; nor do we see often enough the charming flower studies, full of delicacy and feeling, which Mrs. Richard Watson Gilder occasionally gives us. Albertine Randall Wheelan shows great originality, a remarkable sense of the humorous, and a daring handling of the pen.

ETCHING—PORTRAIT OF MRS. PIPER AT SPINNING WHEEL. E. PIPER. ENGLAND.

We enjoy hugely her Chinamen, cats, and other amusing creations. They are real beyond a shadow of a doubt, and one is positive that they have done, and will do again, all the ludicrous things that Mrs. Wheelan represents them as doing.

With the exception of Madelaine Lemaire and a few others, it is difficult to find any women illustrators abroad of much prominence. It sometimes seems that our best magazines, which in accepting only good work have raised illustration to a fine art, have done more toward disseminating a general art culture in the United States than any other single influence.

Now that it is possible to reproduce, by different processes, all kinds of sketches, we find not only pen and ink but lead pencil, crayon, gouache, aquarelle, pastel,

NEEDLEWORK PANEL.
MISS ELIOT WALKER. ENGLAND.

and even oil, rendered with great success. The illustrator has all the delights of using these different mediums and yet working toward a practical result.

Illustration opens so wide and attractive a vista, occupies so high a place in the art of this country, and is withal so remunerative, that women would do well to follow it more largely than they have done heretofore.

A gentleman who is an acknowledged authority on illustration, in lecturing to a class of art students on the pros and cons of working for reproduction, said that to be a successful illustrator one must have, among other qualities, "ingenuity and invention." If this be true of illustration, it applies preëminently to book-cover designing. This particular line of applied arts has received a great

BOOK COVER.
DESIGNED BY SARAH W. WHITMAN.
UNITED STATES

impetus in the last five or six years. Until that time there was practically no attention paid to the proper decoration of book covers. Even the best publishers, except, perhaps, on those rare occasions when an expensive volume was to be issued, were guilty of offering the most preposterous inconsistencies to their patrons.

BOOK COVER, XVI CENTURY.
M. A. SHELDEN. UNITED STATES.

A publisher was quite likely to bring out, let us say, a volume of critical essays with a bunch of daisies thrown across the cover, with a careless disregard of all rules of balance and composition. Among books of a higher character, it was a common thing to find an illustration extracted from the contents of the volume and reproduced on the cover. We hardly know to what to attribute the general revolt among the publishers and the public against this puerile perversion of the art of binding. Perhaps the establishment of such clubs as the Grolier and Aldine has had more to do with the reform in this matter than anything else. Through frequent exhibitions the members of these clubs have been able to study, and, better still, to put before the public, the treasures of private collectors. It was inevitable that the contrast between the beauty of treatment and design seen in the Grolier, Dérome, and kindred styles, and the entire absence of these qualities in the current publications, should be strongly felt. The effect of this influence has been such that publishers have come to realize that a salable book must have an attractive cover. It is not expedient to have hand-tooled leather and such other expensive bits of handicraft as we have inherited from the bibliophiles of the sixteenth and seventeenth centuries, but even in this age of machinery, and the endless publication of cheaply bound books, very charming and artistic cover effects are within the reach of the cultivated and enterprising publisher.

BOOK COVER.
BOSTON
COLLECTION.
UNITED STATES.

Book-cover work presents a wide field, ranging from the thoroughly formal conventional sixteenth-century cover to something appropriate for the so-called railroad novel. It is here that the

Engraved by Rand, McNally & Co.
EASTERN FAÇADE OF THE MINES AND MINING BUILDING,
AS SEEN FROM THE SOUTH.

Engraved by Rand, McNally & Co.

STATUE OF THE REPUBLIC.
By Mr. D. C. French.

THE PERISTYLE.

STATUE OF THE BULL.
By Messrs. E. C. Potter and D. C. French.

illustrator's "ingenuity and invention" is called into play. It is not enough to have a pretty extensive knowledge of historic ornament; she must be able to extract from a book its central idea, and reduce this thought, if possible, to some tangible form permitting a conventional treatment. She must not outrage any true standards of design, yet she should be able to suggest to the casual observer, in a symbolic way, the contents of the volume. Women seem to have a remarkable faculty for designing. Their intuitive sense of decoration, their feeling for beauty of line and harmony of color, insures them a high degree of success. Another consideration is the necessity of rigid, exact treatment of details; uncertain or even suggestive drawing is out of place in cover ornamentation.

BOOK COVER.
ALICE C. MORSE.
UNITED STATES.
By permission of the
Century Co.
(Copyrighted.)

Mrs. Sarah W. Whitman of Boston and Margaret N. Armstrong have taken a firm hold on the publishers, and won recognition from the public, by their appropriate, tasteful, well-studied book decoration.* The designs of Miss Sheldon, Miss Sinclair, and others are promising.

For those possessing the requisite endowment, the ever-widening prospect in cover designing is encouraging.

Just now wood engraving is suffering a temporary eclipse. Its future is problematic, owing to the process-work so much in vogue, and so inimical to the interests of the engraver. It is lamentable to have to admit that there is the slightest question in regard to the future of the wood-cut. It seems impossible that this method of a sympathetic rendering of the artist's idea by a well-trained hand and eye should be superseded by a purely mechanical means in reproduction. We detect, even now, however, symptoms of a reaction toward the old-time wood engraving among the publishers. There are records of women engraving on wood in the time of Albrecht Dürer. Since the revival of the art in England, through the work of Thomas Bewick, we find mention of but one eminent woman engraver, Elizabeth Thompson, daughter of the famous

BOOK COVER.
BOSTON
COLLECTION.
UNITED STATES

---

* Miss Alice C. Morse, the writer of this paper, has made a wide reputation by her excellent and serious work in the designing of book covers.—ED.

engraver John Thompson. Most of our women engravers in this country (and we have many) have sometime been students in a class started by the Cooper Institute about twenty years ago.

Engraving has been taught at the Pennsylvania Academy of Fine Arts also. The Cooper has discontinued the department of wood engraving until the future of the art is assured.

Among the women well worth mentioning for exceptional technical skill are Miss Caroline A. Powell, a former student of the Cooper, and pupil of Timothy Cole. A volume issued by the Society of American Wood Engravers contains fine

BOOK COVER.
SARAH W. WHITMAN.
UNITED STATES.

THE LITTLE KNITTER.
M. O. KOBBÉ. UNITED STATES.
(By permission of the Century
Company—Copyrighted.)

examples of Miss Powell's work. This book was awarded the grand prize at the Berlin International Exposition of Fine Arts. She was the first woman admitted to membership in this society. Since then,

the names of Anna B. Comstock and Edith Cooper have been added. To Miss Powell's earlier achievements she has added some original work.

Mrs. Comstock, the wife of the professor of entomology at Cornell, has made a specialty of engraving moths, beetles, etc., to illustrate her husband's books. Her

ANTWERP PEASANT.
M. O. KOBBÉ. UNITED STATES.
(By permission of the Century
Company—Copyrighted.)

AUNT TABITHA.
M. O. KOBBÉ. UNITED STATES.
(By permission of the Century
Company—Copyrighted.)

work in this direction is remarkable. Edith Cooper is well known to lovers of wood engraving through the pages of the magazines.

Alice Barber Stevens, before she became prominent as an illustrator, did some good wood engraving.

Miss Waldeyer excels in fac-simile. We have also the Misses Naylor, thoroughly good all-round workers and engravers; Miss Berger, and others.

The mechanical difficulties of wood engraving are great, and can only be overcome by the closest application. As the standard, too, is very high here, there is no encouragement to young workers in the existing order of things. Unless there is a change for the better, we shall soon find ourselves without competent engravers to fill the places of the older ones as they leave the ranks.

PEN AND INK DRAWING—"KITTENS AT SCHOOL."
A. R. WHEELAN. UNITED STATES. By permission of the Century Co. (Copyrighted.)

The future of the wood-cut lies perhaps almost entirely in the direction of original work, or reproductive engraving of marked individual excellence.

Fortunately, even the best process-work does not, in many cases, give the effect necessary, and a wood engraver of unusual ability is assured abundant opportunity for the exercise of his or her calling.

As women increase in physical vigor and mental grasp—through the higher education—they eagerly seek an outlet for their energies. In art, perhaps, more than in any other profession, do they find the conditions which make for success.

ALICE C. MORSE.

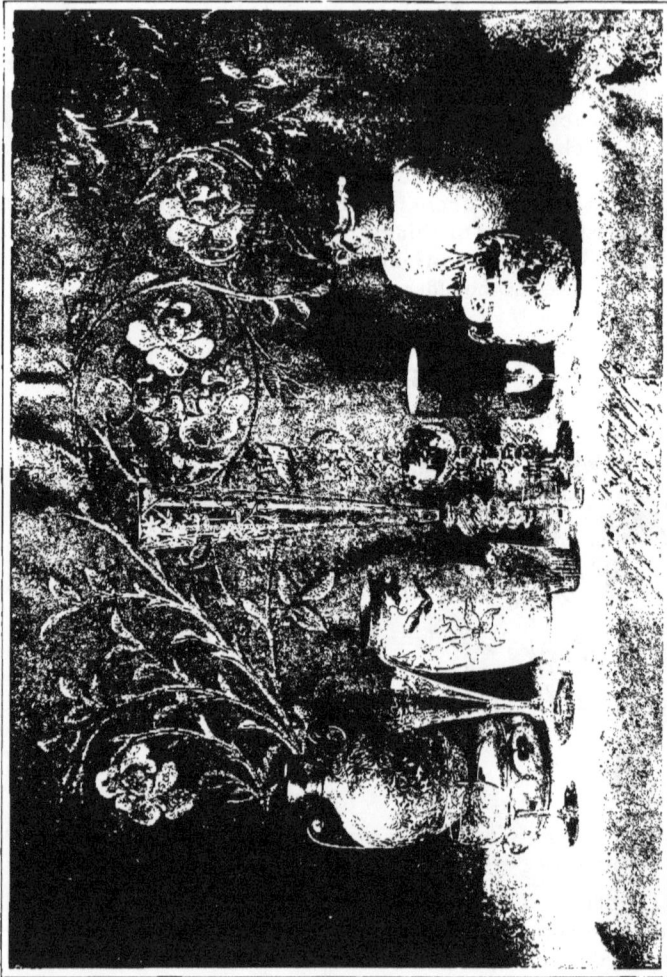

POTTERY. CINCINNATI COLLECTION. UNITED STATES.

THE WORK OF CINCINNATI WOMEN IN DECORATED POTTERY.

THE ceramic exhibit by the women of Cincinnati, as shown in the Cincinnati Room at the Columbian Exposition, is one of the results of an impulse which, in 1874-75, was felt by some of the leading potters of the United States and by a few women in different localities. There was no concerted action between the potters and the women, and none between the women of Cincinnati and those of other cities.

These sporadic symptoms seemed to indicate that the times were ripe for the introduction of a new industry into the country, an industry that recommended itself to the taste of many women, and seemed to offer a profitable field of future work for them.

When the women of Cincinnati began their experiments there was no available knowledge in reference to the art of deco-

POTTERY. CINCINNATI COLLECTION. UNITED STATES.

rating, and no suitable kilns for firing their wares. The first result of their efforts worthy of note was a collection of overglaze decoration sent by them to the Centennial Exposition in 1876. Of this collection, two tea-cups and saucers and a chocolate pitcher, loaned by the Cincinnati Museum, will be found in the Cincinnati Room.

In 1877 experiments were made in the common clays of the neighborhood, in incised and relief work, and in the use of color in the biscuit, a first step in advance of overglaze decoration.

PAINTED PORCELAIN VASE, OLD SWEDISH STYLE. HELENE HOLD. SWEDEN.

A few notable pieces of this early underglaze decoration from the museum may also be seen. These pieces, when they appeared, seemed marvelous to us, and perhaps no achievement since made has marked so great a step in advance. The pieces representing this period are three small plates, showing the first success in this underglaze, and a large vase, white body, fishes, and water-plants.

A later piece may be mentioned in this connection, a punch-bowl, yellow body, with dragon.

These enthusiastic women, believing in themselves, and foreseeing in the future work for many hands, brought clays from distant parts of the State and built suitable kilns for their firing.

A pottery club was organized in 1879, which has been one of the active instrumentalities in the advancement of many branches of decorative work. The decoration of the Pottery Club shows some of the best work of Cincinnati women. Miss McLaughlin, president of this club, discovered the decorative process of the Limoges Faience, specimens of which will be found in the exhibit of the Cincinnati Pottery Club. Mrs. Bellamy Storer was early in the field of decoration a n d experiments; her talents were varied and her taste individual.

The work of the ladies was, much of it, fired, and their experiments made at one of t h e leading · potteries, where some simple arrangements were made for their accommodation. The progress of the work soon outgrew the facilities afforded at the pottery, and in the autumn

POTTERY. CINCINNATI COLLECTION. UNITED STATES.

of 1880 Mrs. Storer established her own pottery in one of the suburbs. The success of " Rookwood Pottery," both in an artistic and a commercial sense, may be regarded as the most perfect realization of decorative art in clay in the United States; the result of a woman's taste, skill, and perseverance, from the initial step until it reached a period of commercial success. Mrs. Storer's

POTTERY. CINCINNATI COLLECTION. UNITED STATES.

judgment led her to select those whose experience was greater than her own in perfecting her manufacture. The decorators, from the first, were pupils of the School of Design, and perhaps in the application of artistic principles to an industry the influence of the school has been as noticeably shown here as in any other direction.

Mrs. Storer herself, at intervals of leisure from her many engagements, continues to practice her favorite art of decoration, and

POTTERY AND GLASS—CINCINNATI COLLECTION. UNITED STATES.

her work will be shown in the Cincinnati Room. Her taste is inclined to the grotesque, and especially to the Japanese in style. She is reported to have said: "If any one thinks my dragons are not anatomically correct, let him prove it."

While Mrs. Storer was developing and perfecting her pottery, the Pottery Club, and many women outside of it, were as busily engaged in the various branches of potting and porcelain decoration.

Perhaps no work done in Cincinnati seems more individual than that of Mrs. C. A. Plimpton, in the common clays of Ohio. Her artistic taste early led her to see the adaptability of these soft clays to decorative uses. Her processes consisted in inlaying contrasting colors in the green clay; in relief work in a variety of shades of clay; and of " pâte-sur-pâte," or ship decoration, in landscape and other effects, ranging in color from dark-brown clays, through the reds, to yellow and white. Interesting specimens of her work, loaned by individuals and by the Cincinnati Museum, will be found in the Cincinnati Room.

In the limits assigned to this paper, it is impossible to do more than allude in a brief manner to the work of Cincinnati women in this interesting specialty. Specimens of the very early work, of the first successes in color under the glaze, of early Rookwood, and indeed of all branches through the days of experiment and uncertainty down to and including the finished work of the most experienced hands of the present day, will be found in the Cincinnati Room.

It is an interesting circumstance that the women who began the work in 1875 are, with few exceptions, still engaged in it.

It can not be doubted from the results of the past few years that there is an interesting future in pottery for decorative art in Cincinnati. The variety and beauty of the common clays of Ohio are great, and the success thus far in their use for decorative purposes is such as to warrant the expectation that the field in that direction is, as yet, barely entered upon.

Perhaps at no center of pottery work in the country is more originality and variety in work to be found than in Cincinnati. Nowhere have the common clays been used in such variety of combination and decoration, nor has so much effect been produced by colored and contrasting glazes.

ELIZABETH W. PERRY.

WOMAN IN SCIENCE.

HE mind of woman has always shown itself in sympathy
with the harmony and beauty of the physical universe. In
the pursuit of knowledge she often elects as her favorite
paths those which bring her into close relations with nature. Her
proverbial propensity to investigate, her acknowledged patience,
her delicacy of manipulation, her exactness of detail all find legitimate scope in the nice observation and conscientious work of the
laboratory. With advancing
education, better equipped
than ever before, she re-
sponds to the appeal of
natural forms and pro-
cesses. Her eye, and ear,
and touch become sensitive,
her mental perception keen
to note variations of type
and modifications of structure.

It is pleasing to record
that American women of
this generation are entering
the various departments of
scientific research with enthusiastic devotion.

While college doors
were yet closed to the sex,
the modern movement for
freeing woman from the
traditional limitations not
having been inaugurated,

WATER-COLOR.
JESSUP COLLECTION OF NORTH AMERICAN WOODS.
MINNIE R. SARGENT. UNITED STATES.

individual women were often led to study in a more or less
isolated way for their own satisfaction. How many herbari-
ums, portfolios of drawings of plant or animal forms, collec-

(107)

Engraved by Rand, McNally & Co.

THE UNITED STATES GOVERNMENT AND MANUFACTURES BUILDINGS.

SIZE OF THE FORMER, 350 x 420 FEET. ARCHITECT, MR. W. J. EDBROOKE. COST, $725,000.

OLD ENGLISH CLOCK IN CARVED WOOD CASE. MRS. ELIOT. ENGLAND.

INTERIOR OF AGRICULTURAL BUILDING, AS SEEN FROM THE WESTERN GALLERY.

Engraved by Rand, McNally & Co.

tions of shells, sea-mosses, and minerals have been stored away as private memorials of happy research and experimentation! Field and forest, mountain and shore have been explored for treasures of science, by many a modest daughter of the soil or darling of luxury. A few of these early students, lifted into prominence by the persistency and value of their work, grace the record of woman's intellectual achievement with a fame which we are proud to acknowledge.

Maria Mitchell as a discoverer in astronomical science is a peeress of the realm in that exalted branch of research. A student from childhood with her father, an astronomer of repute, she watched from his observatory at Nantucket the suns and planets in their majestic march through the stellar spaces; she took observations, computed orbits, recorded celestial phenomena, resolved nebulæ, studied sun-spots, the satellites of Jupiter and Saturn, the color of stars, and prepared the American Nautical Almanac for many years, till October, 1847, she hailed a new comet which "swam into her ken." For this discovery she received a gold medal from the King of Denmark and a copper medal from the republic of San Marino. Miss Mitchell

POTTERY—CINCINNATI COLLECTION. UNITED STATES. was the first woman elected to the American Academy of Arts and Sciences. She was appointed Professor of Astronomy at Vassar College on the opening of that institution, and later visited Europe, where she was the honored guest of Sir John Herschel, of Humboldt, and of Le Verrier. Her unaffected and unpretentious personality, as well as her honest and sober self-respect, made her a valued friend of great scientists everywhere. She received the degree of LL. D. from Hanover in 1882, and from Columbia in 1887. She died January

28, 1889, illustrious through her contributions to science, and honored in the hearts of all her countrywomen.

The name of Miss Eliza A. Youmans is conspicuous as a pioneer in the field of botany. She wrote a treatise upon plant-life which marked an era in methods of study and teaching. Hers was one of the first books which pursued object-teaching as the true method, and made original observation the basis of investigation. She was the sister of Professor Youmans of New York, and was associated with her father in his intercourse with the scientists of Europe.

In many high-schools for girls, private seminaries for women, normal schools, or advanced private academies, the natural sciences of geography, geology, astronomy, botany, and zoölogy have been long taught by women with distinguished ability. Now the colleges for women maintain professorships in every branch of science filled honorably and successfully by women. Consult the catalogues of these institutions for their names, flanked by degrees and titles witnessing their learning and their achievements.

Even in the universities themselves young women wrest honors in the scientific field from

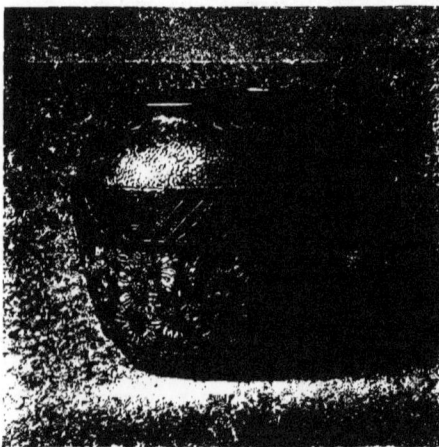

POTTERY—CINCINNATI COLLECTION. UNITED STATES.

the most ardent champions of the other sex; the increasing fellowships for young women are leading forward the most gifted and the most ambitious of our girl graduates to higher attainments, year by year, and there are wider opportunities of competition, not only in the physical and natural sciences, but in ethnology, archæology, philology, psychology, and even distinctive branches and special lines of applied science.

There is, moreover, a vast amount of work of a high order and great value done by women as assistants in the scientific departments of our universities. The Harvard observatory and Harvard botanical and zoölogical museums testify to the thoroughness and comprehensiveness of such assistance in observing, recording, and comparing phenomena, and in the exacting details of microscopy, photography, and spectroscopy, as well as in making up monographs and arranging and classifying the collections. The Natural History Society and the Marine Biological Laboratory of Massachusetts are greatly dependent on the active assistance and original investigation of women as students and co-workers with the curators and professors. A number of women are catalogued in various parts of the country as curators of museums, as instructors or professors of science in the institutes and colleges, and as deans of faculty. Mrs. Ellen H. Richards of the Massachusetts Institute of Technology, in the department of sanitary chemistry, is widely known. Mrs. Rachel Lloyd of Lincoln, Neb., one of the most noted women in chemistry in this country, took her degree at Zurich. Mrs. Katharine Brandegee of California Academy of Science is curator of a botanical museum. Emily Gregory, Ph. D., of Barnard College, is recognized in botany. Rachel L. Bodley made a catalogue of natural history which was regarded by Prof. Asa Gray as a valuable contribution to science. She filled the chair of

WATER-COLOR. JESSUP COLLECTION OF NORTH AMERICAN WOODS. MINNIE R. SARGENT. UNITED STATES.

chemistry and toxology in the Woman's Medical College of Pennsylvania, and became dean of the faculty. She died in 1888. Mrs. Louisa Reed Stowell, who has been in charge of the botanical laboratory of Michigan University for twelve years, is a member of the Royal Microscopic Society of London, and of many other scientific bodies. She has made over a hundred contributions to current scientific literature, all illustrated by original drawings from her own microscopical preparations. At the Boston Institute of Technology the Margaret Cheney Reading Room keeps in memory the promise of a fair young life happily devoted to the pursuit of chemistry. Grace Anna Lewis of Pennsylvania is well known as an authority on the habits of birds, and has lectured on this subject with great

8

BRONZE PLATE. MARCELLE LANCELOT-CROCE. FRANCE.

acceptance. Miss Cora Clarke of Jamaica Plain has made an exhaustive collection of galls, fungi, and mosses; Mrs. Lemmon, artist of the California Board of Forestry; Miss Marion Talbot of Chicago University, department of domestic science; and a host of others who fill responsible positions in all departments of science might swell the list far beyond the purpose or limits of this paper.

The department of biology seems to attract a large proportion of recent students, who meet the demands of laboratory work with great efficiency. The science of ethnology has been ably served by Miss Alice C. Fletcher of Massachusetts. She studied the archæological remains of the Ohio and Mississippi valleys, and went in 1881 to live among the Omaha Indians, under the auspices of the Peabody Museum of Archæology, for the further pursuit of archæ-

ology and ethnology. She has contributed results of great value, covering Indian traditions, customs, religious ceremonies, and many kindred subjects. She published a book on "Indian Civilization and Education" in 1886, and was then sent to Alaska to investigate the condition of the natives. She is now engaged in making allotments of land to the Omaha Indians, for which service she was appointed by the Government.

The scientific literature of women is becoming very ex-

WATER COLOR.
H. R. H. PRINCESS LOUISE, OF DENMARK.

tended. From the text-books of Mrs. Emma Willard and Mrs. Horace Mann, of Mrs. Louis Agassiz and Mrs. Richards, of Miss Crocker and Miss Arms, to the charming sketches of Olive Thorne Miller, we have a constantly increasing series of elementary works in natural science. The books of Miss Jane Newell of Cambridge, on botany; of Miss Julia McNair Wright, on plant and animal life, a series called "Seaside and Wayside," with other small but significant volumes intended to meet the popular interest and comprehension and arouse a love of scientific study, are pouring daily from the press.* The department of Elementary Science, or

---

* Mrs. Hopkins, the writer of this paper, is the author of " Educational Psychology," " A Hand-Book of the Earth," "Observation Lessons," " Elementary Science," etc.—ED.

ENAMELED GLASS. ELLA CASELLA. ENGLAND.

Natural Study, in the common schools is almost wholly in the hands of women as supervisors and teachers, and it can not be questioned that it is directed and presented with remarkable adaptation to the general need and the fostering of scientific methods of study, as well as a love of nature.

Directly in the line of pure science is Mrs. Mary Hemenway's undertaking in the department of archæology. Her southwestern archæological expedition, with its resulting museum, literature, and historical collections, is an invaluable foundation for future ethnological research, and is fruitful already of great results for the original study of American history. The collection accruing to the expedition and investigations thus far has been recently exhibited in Madrid, and proved prolific of results for so short a period. It is hoped that some permanent establishment of this museum of American archæology may be effected for the emulation of such noble scientific work as that of the late eminent Egyptologist, Miss Amelia B. Edwards.

It is impossible to convey an adequate idea of the promise of all these signs of the times in this brief résumé. It seems fitting that some flower of scientific expression, some emblem of the spirit of womanhood beautifying even the dry technicalities of the theme, should bring this paper to a close. We find this in a series of four hundred and twelve water-color paintings by Mrs. Charles S. Sargent of Brookline, prepared to illustrate the Jessup collection of North American woods in the American Museum of Natural History of New York, for a volume written and furnished by her husband. These illustrations are drawn from nature, the size of life, and for outline, color, grace, beauty, and scientific detail they are beyond criticism. Professor Goodale of Harvard University declares them to be unique and admirable in the realm of both science and art; the very spirit of the trees stirs in them, and a revelation of beauty and harmony greets us in these inimitable and loving studies from nature. Mrs. Sargent's drawings take the place in the delineation of native foliage that Audubon's matchless and exhaustive sketches hold in the representation of the birds of North America.

May we not assure ourselves that whatever woman's thought and study shall embrace will thereby receive a new inspiration; that she will save science from materialism, and art from a gross realism; that the "eternal womanly shall lead upward and onward?"

LOUISA PARSONS HOPKINS.

FAC-SIMILE OF BIBLE BELONGING TO QUEEN ELIZABETH.
ROYAL SOCIETY OF ART NEEDLEWORK. ENGLAND.

WOMAN IN LITERATURE.

IN this great review of ours, each company in turn steps to the front, shows its colors, salutes, and passes on to make room for the next. Painters, sculptors, needlewomen, have gone by, and now the woman of letters must raise her banner (sable, a pen rampant by two ink-pots couchant, on a white ground; motto, "Legion!"), must come forward, and give an account of herself.

She is notoriously modest, yet she thinks she has a pretty good account to render, and points with gentle pride to her well-ordered ranks; while, to convince the world of her advance, she refers the public to the literary women of half a century ago, and challenges a comparison. Though she boasts of no higher attainment than her sisters of other professions, yet she may say that she comes of an older family; for woman began to write before she thought of taking prominence in other arts. Was not Anne Bradstreet, wife of Simon the Governor, the first American poet? She died in 1672. She was called the Tenth Muse, and the grim Puritans wept over her poems. One reads them to-day with respect, but feels no keen desire for her Parnassus. Next in order, perhaps, comes Miss Hannah Adams, a gentle and lovely soul, who lived into our own century, and, dying, was the first person buried in Mount Auburn. The family of Sedgwick gives us two writers in the same generation, though one of them held the name by marriage only, having been a Livingston by birth. This latter was Susan, author of several novels and tales, of which one, "Walter Thornby," was written when she was over seventy years of age. Better known than this persevering lady was her sister-in-law, Miss Catherine Sedgwick, whose moral tales attained a wide popularity. She might be called the American Miss Edgeworth, and some of her titles, "The Poor Rich Man and the Rich Poor Man," "Means and Ends," etc., remind us forcibly of that sprightly moralist.

Next we must mention Mrs. Sigourney, a writer of wide repute, though little read to-day. "Pocahontas and Other Poems," "Lays of the Heart," "Tales in Prose and Verse," the very titles breathe of bygone days and thoughts; yet Mrs. Sigourney was a noble and lovely woman, and one might spend an hour much less profitably than in making or renewing acquaintance with her writings.

In looking back at these early lights, we must not forget the Davidson sisters, Lucretia and Margaret, that lovely pair whose story was so touchingly and beautifully told by Washington Irving.

WALL HANGING REPRESENTING THE GODDESS BONOMIE.
FIGURE BY BURNE-JONES, BELONGING TO THE ROYAL SCHOOL OF ART NEEDLEWORK.
ENGLAND.

It is a sad little story of too early development, hectic beauty and blossoming, and death by consumption almost before womanhood was attained. Lucretia, poor child, wrote 278 poems, and died at seventeen. Margaret's record is scarcely less startling and painful.

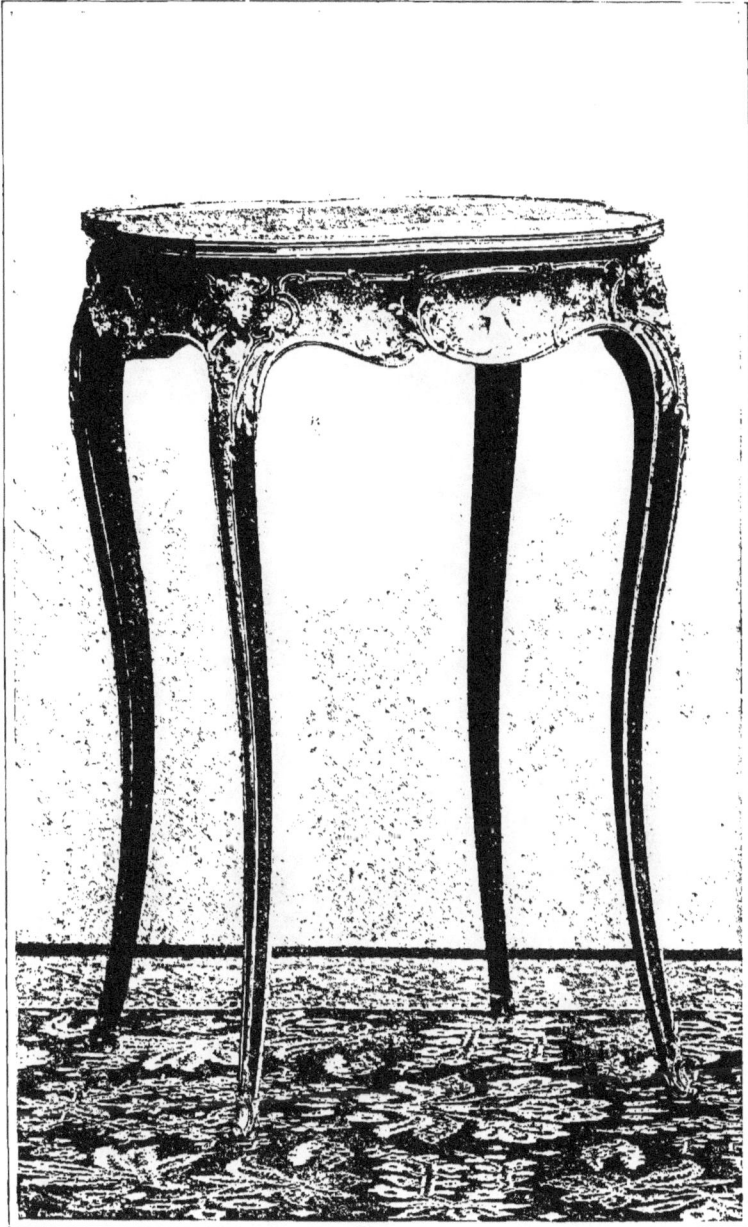

LOUIS XV. TABLE. DECORATIONS BY MME. G. NIETER. FRANCE.

One wishes they might have lived to-day, and have had some chance of rounding out their gentle lives.

Next we have Mrs. Frances Osgood, author of " A Wreath of Flowers from New England," and other volumes of poetry; and, contemporary with her, the commanding figure of Margaret Fuller. It would be pleasant to dwell at some length on the life of this amazing woman, who began to write Latin verses at eight years

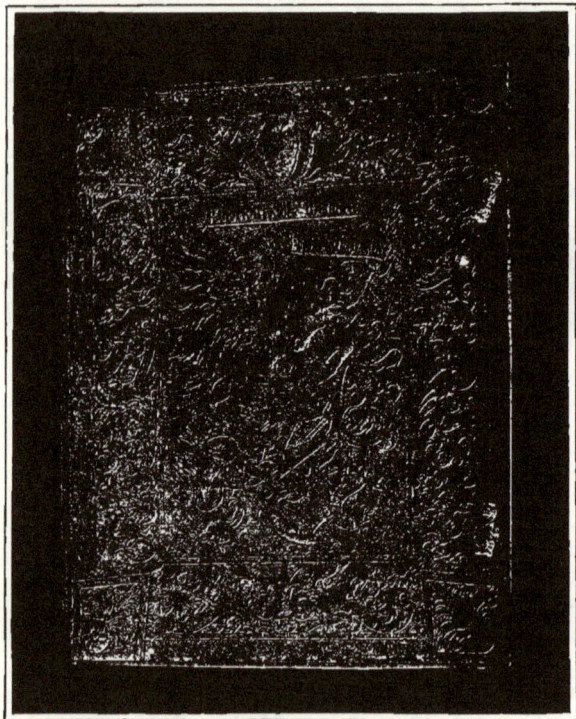

PORTFOLIO CONTAINING PORTRAITS OF DISTINGUISHED
SWEDISH WOMEN.

old, and whose powers were at their height when the fatal storm of July 16, 1850, hurried her, with all she loved, to her ocean grave; but this brief record can do little more than mention names and dates, and those who do not know Queen Margaret's story are prayed to read it, in Mrs. Howe's memoir of her.

Lydia Maria Child was older than either of the two last-named

THE CART-HORSE GROUP. NORTH SIDE MAIN BASIN.

BY MESSRS. E. C. POTTER AND D. C. FRENCH.

THE SOUTH POND.

Engraved by Rand, McNally & Co.

ladies, having been born in 1802; but her beautiful and helpful life was a long one, closing only in 1880, so that we may think of her as a link between the old time and the new. Her name is inseparably connected with the anti-slavery movement, and she was for many years editor of the *National Anti-Slavery Standard*. In other fields of literature, her " History of Rome " won her deserved renown, while the lovely romance of "Philothea" is still read with pleasure by young and old.

So far we have dealt only with those who have won their promotion and passed on from this field of work to another; but the next name on the roll of honor is that of one who is still living, the dean of American literary women, Mrs. Harriet Beecher Stowe. Nearly half a century has passed since the world was electrified by the publication of "Uncle Tom's Cabin." The quiet, hard-working wife of the country parson and professor found herself suddenly famous—raised to a height of popularity which might well have turned a less strong and sensible head; but one does not learn that Mrs. Stowe was ever unduly elated by her popularity, or that either hardship or prosperity could shake the serene composure of her mind. Of late years

CARVED WOOD AND LEATHER CHAIR.
MADE BY H. R. H. THE PRINCESS OF WALES. ENGLAND.

she has laid down the pen, and passes her days quietly at home, devoting much time to the flowers she loves so fondly.

Gladly as we hold the thought that Mrs. Stowe is still with us in the land of our sojourn, it is none the less true that she belongs to the last period of literature, not to the present. It is in the figure of Mrs. Julia Ward Howe that we must greet the foremost literary woman of to-day. Though she has long years to look back upon, Mrs. Howe is still wholly of the present, and her clear eyes look forward with intelligent comprehension to the future. She was born in 1819, the daughter of Samuel Ward, a New York merchant of the old stately school. A student all her life, a writer from early childhood, it was not till some years after her marriage that she thought of publishing any of her work.

She has told the writer how, when she was perhaps nineteen years of age, she showed some of her poems to Margaret Fuller, at the request of a mutual friend. Miss Fuller was delighted with them, and eagerly advised Miss Ward to have them

CARVED WOOD AND LEATHER STOOL.
PRINCESS VICTORIA OF WALES. ENGLAND.

published. Mrs. Howe still remembers the shock this suggestion gave her. It was still considered "singular" for a woman to publish her writings. It was out of the question for Mr. Ward's daughter to think of such a thing; it seemed a pity that Miss Fuller should even have suggested it, so the maiden thought at the time. Meanwhile the word was spoken, the seed dropped, to germinate in its own good time, and blossom in unfading beauty. Her work is so well known that it is unnecessary to allude to it in detail. From the publication of "Passion Flowers," in 1853, down to the present day, her pen has never been idle, her voice never silent in the cause of progress and of practical Christianity. May it be long before we cease to follow the course of that active pen, to listen to that silver voice!

In her own generation Mrs. Howe stands nearly alone among literary women in this country. Fanny Kemble was of her time, and, though not of us, was for so many years with us that we may

SEAT OF STOOL IN LEATHER WORK. PRINCESS VICTORIA OF WALES. ENGLAND.

perhaps place her name upon our roll. Mrs. Kemble's "Records of a Girlhood" and "Records of Later Life" will always be read with delight; and she has also given us some tender and graceful poems. That brilliant and eventful life ended, as is well known, but a few weeks ago. Another contemporary of Mrs. Howe's is Mrs. Edna D. Cheney, whose work will be spoken of later.

First among that great feminine army of translators who trans-

plant the flowers of foreign thought into the garden of our literature, stands Miss Katherine Wormly, whose admirable translations
of Balzac have introduced the great French novelist to a new world
of readers.

Mrs. James T. Fields has written all too little, to speak from
the standpoint of our wishes, yet we have some delightful things
from her pen—a volume of poems, " Under the Olives"; "Asphodel,"
a romance, and the charming reminiscences of famous men, which
have appeared from time to time in the magazines, are enough to
make us all cry for
more; yet we are glad
and grateful for these.
Mrs. Fields is a promi-
nent figure of literary
Boston, and there is
no house more de-
lightful than hers.

But now the plot
thickens. There came
a day when it no long-
er was singular for
women to write. Sud-
denly it came, one
hardly knew how; the
windows of the House
of Woman were
thrown open, and in-
stead of here and
there a single lonely
watcher on the roof
was a crowd of women
leaning out, greeting
the fresh air with

CARVED WOOD AND LEATHER STOOL.
PRINCESS MAUD OF WALES. ENGLAND.

rapture, eager to see, to hear, and more especially to tell. From
this moment I drop all attempt at chronological arrangement as
invidious; indeed, I can do little more than mention the names
that come thronging to my mind. The living must give place to
those who have passed from our knowledge.

Helen Hunt, a name beloved by all, has slept for many years
beneath her cairn in the West; Emily Dickinson, dying unknown,
left us the afterglow of her strange, secluded, seething life. Even
as I write, the bells are tolling for the sweet New England poetess

and noble woman, Lucy Larcom, whose peaceful life has ended peacefully not many months after that of her friend, John Green-leaf Whittier. Her "New England Girlhood" gives us glimpses of a life that it is good to know about, to remember, in these days when luxury and the love of it grow too fast upon us; and some of her poems find an honored place in every anthology of American poets.

How long is it since Louisa Alcott died? four years, or four weeks? Her memory is so fresh in our minds it is hard to realize the flight of time. One seldom sees a fresh copy of her works; they

SEAT OF STOOL IN LEATHER WORK. PRINCESS MAUD OF WALES. ENGLAND.

are always read to pieces, thumbed by eager schoolgirls, marked with enthusiastic pencilings, which the guardians of libraries try in vain to prevent. But widely popular as her stories are, we feel that the woman herself was finer than anything she wrote; and the heroic figure pictured so ably and so lovingly in Mrs. Cheney's admirable life of Miss Alcott is but feebly shadowed forth in her own writings.

Mrs. Louise Chandler Moulton has given us several volumes of poems and some charming stories, of which one set in particular,

9

the " Nightcap " series, is recalled by the writer with tender affec-
tion. Mrs. Rebecca Harding Davis has written little of late years,
but her powerful novels have won her an enduring place in literature. Miss Constance Fenimore Woolson, to whom we owe the joy
of " East Angels," not to be forgotten; Mrs. Whitney, Elizabeth
Stuart Phelps, Gail Hamilton, Celia Thaxter, Harriet Prescott
Spofford, Elizabeth Stoddard—this is degenerating into a mere catalogue; but what is a poor scribe to do, who is limited to so many
words, and who sees ever new files passing before her, pen in hand,
laurel on brow, waving the foolscap banner? I would fain dwell
on each of these honored names, but must pass on to others no less
worthy of honor. Mrs. Burnett, to whom the crown of the children's love has been given since Miss Alcott laid it down; Mrs. Van
Rensselaer, Mrs. Burton Harrison, "Susan Coolidge," Kate Doug-
las Wiggin, Mary Hallock Foote, and those sweet singers, Edith
Thomas and Helen Gray Cone. A step further and we greet Mrs.
Deland, "Charles Egbert Craddock," and those three who string
jewels on a golden thread, the queens of the short story, Miss
Jewett, Miss Wilkins, and Octave Thanet.

Following these come Maud Howe Elliott and Louise Imogen
Guiney, Amelie Rives, Agnes Repplier, and Chicago's poetess,
Harriet Monroe.

But now I can no more; and I feel as the hostess does who has
tried to invite all her acquaintance to an entertainment. If it is
only in this last breath that I speak of Mary Hartwell Catherwood
and Elizabeth Cavazza; if it is only now that I greet the sweet memory of Emma Lazarus, that flower of Israel—it is not because I
honor them less, but because the human brain has limits, while the
number of women of letters to-day has none.

Greeting to one and all, and love, and honor; those whom I
have left out, sitting at the world's great feast, will not miss the
spoonful of victuals that I unwittingly deny them; those of whom I
have spoken will pardon the brief and insufficient mention.

And so, roll-call being over, the Literary Brigade shoulders
pens, raises the banner once more, and passes on.

LAURA E. RICHARDS.

THE LAGOON DURING A REGATTA,

LOOKING NORTHEAST TOWARD THE FISHERIES BUILDING.

Engraved by Rand, McNally & Co.

ELECTRICITY BUILDING.

SIZE, 700 x 350 FEET. ARCHITECTS, MESSRS. VAN BRUNT & HOWE. COST, $410,000.

THE LIBRARY.

O NE of the most important features of the Woman's Building is the library, which contains the writings of American and foreign women. The work of collecting the American books was done by committees in the different States. Various plans were pursued in making these collections. Massachusetts held that quality, rather than quantity, was to be sought. A high standard of excellence was required, and in most cases the authors were only invited to send one of their works. The chairman of this committee, Margaret Deland, herself our leading woman novelist, prepared a very excellent catalogue, which accompanied Massachusetts' small and valuable exhibit. This catalogue includes 2,000 books, written by Massachusetts women between the years of 1612 and 1893. It will therefore be seen that while the Bay State might have sent 2,000 books, she contented herself with sending one hundred.

As New York has made the largest collection, a statement of the plan pursued by its literary committee has been prepared by the chairman. The library is an exhibit rather than a working library, and the catalogue, which has been very carefully prepared, will prove one of its most interesting features. The arrangement of the shelves shows the number of books sent by the different States and countries, so that, at a glance, the visitor may see that Belgium is well represented, and that France, Germany, and Great Britain lead among the foreign collections; that New Hampshire has given itself very little trouble, and New York a great deal. The cata-

PAINTING—"A SELLREIN WOMAN."
BARONESS MARIANNE ESCHENBURG.
AUSTRIA.

logue is so arranged that a very cursory examination will show the subjects with which women writers have chiefly dealt. An index of authors gives many details of each writer's professional life,

BLACK AND WHITE ILLUSTRATION—"IN THE MEETING HOUSE."
A. B. STEPHENS. UNITED STATES.

showing the line of work to which she has devoted herself, and any honors that she may have won.

The English books deserve careful examination. They are accompanied by some very valuable manuscripts; among others we may see the handwriting of Maria Edgeworth, Miss Burney, Jane

Austin, Mrs. Gaskell, Charlotte Brönté, and George Eliot. The first page of Adam Bede, with an affectionate note of dedication to George Lewes, signed Marian Lewes, dated 1859, is one of the most interesting objects in the World's Fair. In the same case with these precious manuscripts may be seen three fine editions of the " Boke of St. Albans," by Dame Juliana Berners.

Germany has been wonderfully generous to us, and her 500 admirably selected and beautifully bound volumes are a gift from the women of Germany.

Spain sends us a treasure of old and rare books and priceless manuscripts.

Bohemia has 307 volumes, and France 800.

One of the valuable features of the collection in our library is the large number of pamphlets and monographs on professional and scientific subjects. All women who have published papers of this description are earnestly invited to send copies of their work to the librarian of the Woman's Building. The visitor will find volumes written by women from Japan, Turkey, Finland, Sweden, Italy, Germany, France, Bohemia, Belgium, Cuba, Peru, and Austria, and one volume in Arabic, by an American missionary. Many of the States and countries represented have given their collection to the Library of Woman's Work, which is to be established in the permanent Woman's Building, to the erection of which all who have labored for our building look forward.

A card catalogue of the books, which now number 7,000, is being arranged, under the direction of Miss Edith E. Clarke. No author who has examined the careful and beautiful arrangement of the catalogue would be satisfied to remain unrepresented in it. We earnestly beg all women writers, who have not already done so, to contribute their books on whatever subject.

In this connection it seems well to call attention to the very large field of work which opens for women as librarians. There is no department of human labor for which our American girls are better fitted than to the careful, patient, exact profession of the librarian. Mr. Melville Dewey of the State Library at Albany gives, as the result of his experience, the statement that our young women are better fitted for this work than their brothers. We learn from him that there is an ever-increasing demand for women librarians.

Owing to the unavoidable delay attending the arrangement of the library, it has been impossible to secure the necessary data for the preparation of an article which does justice to this most

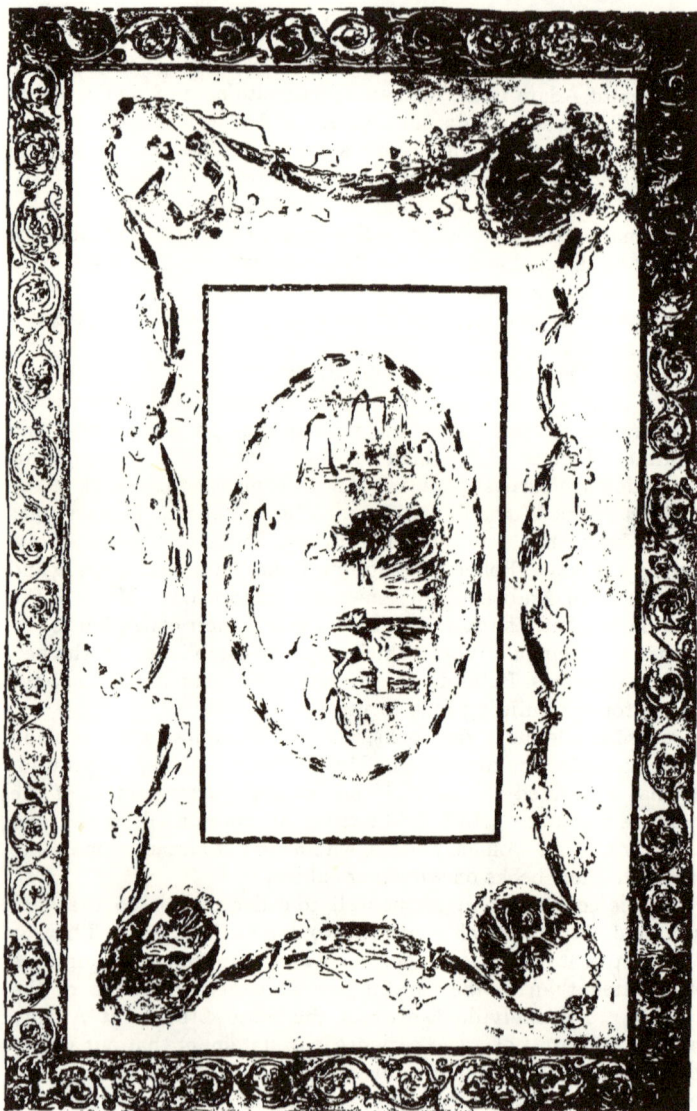

CEILING OF LIBRARY. DORA WHEELER KEITH, UNITED STATES.

important department. These few rough notes, made when our volume is already in press, are entirely inadequate to the subject. They are made in the hope that they may call the attention of the visitor to a most interesting and valuable feature of our building.

The following statement of the number of books received at our library was made on the 30th day of May, 1893:

Alabama	64	Mississippi	4	Washington	
Alaska		Missouri	3	West Virginia	5
Arizona		Montana		Wisconsin	4
Arkansas	1	Nebraska	20	Wyoming	
California	9	Nevada		Arabia	
Colorado	46	New Hampshire	3	Belgium	350
Connecticut	111	New Jersey	350	Bohemia	307
Delaware	8	New Mexico		Cuba (included in Spain).	
District of Columbia	100	New York	2,500	Denmark	
Florida	8	North Carolina	26	Finland	1
Georgia	9	North Dakota		France	800
Idaho		Ohio	96	Germany (gift)	500
Illinois	100	Oregon	11	Great Britain	500
Indiana	1	Pennsylvania	400	Italy (gift — more are coming)	150
Iowa	2	Rhode Island	45		
Kansas	3	South Carolina	13	Japan	50
Kentucky	6	South Dakota		Mexico	9
Louisiana	72	Tennessee		Peru	1
Maine	42	Texas	27	Portugal	
Maryland	56	Utah		Spain	300
Massachusetts	100	Vermont		Sweden	130
Michigan	24	Virginia	14	Turkey	1
Minnesota	34				

THE EDITOR.

DESIGNS FOR LACE. NINA FRENCH. UNITED STATES.

LANDSCAPE —"BANKS OF THE OKA." MLLE. OLSOUFIEFF. RUSSIA.

NEW YORK LITERARY EXHIBIT.

THE chairman of the Committee on Literature of the Board of Women Managers of the State of New York has organized and instituted an exhibit differing somewhat in character from any other in the library. It contains three departments: First, women's work in the writing and translating of books; second, their work in literary clubs and classes; and third, their work in journalism and in periodical literature.

The collection of books, which numbers 2,400 volumes, was made by the Wednesday Afternoon Club of New York, which contributed $1,000 to this end. We have attempted to make an historic, chronologic collection of all the books ever written by women either residents or natives of the State

SEAL OF NEW YORK STATE BOARD.
LYDIA EMMET. (Copyrighted.)

of New York. It is believed that this will prove of benefit to future students of literature and lovers of Americana. It is a collection limited both by sex and locality, but valuable because of its completeness within these limits. The Committee of the Wednesday Afternoon Club, under the efficient chairmanship of Mrs. Frederick Ferris Thompson, aided by Mrs. Charles Royce, Miss Willard, Mrs. Richard Ewart, Mrs. Alfred Corning Clark, Mrs. Junius

Henri Browne, and others, with the special support and aid of Mrs. Runkle, the brilliant literary critic of New York and the president of the club, has done a very thorough and exhaustive work. Great assistance has been rendered by the committees in each county of the State, by several of the well-known publishers, and by most of the authors represented. The collection contains children's books, works of fiction, science, cookery, and household economics, education, language, translation, original verse, compiled verse, travels, biography, his-

CARVED OAK MIRROR FRAME. MISS REEKS. ENGLAND.

tory, art, and religion. The oldest book is a novel, "The Female Quixote," by Charlotte Ramsay Lennox, who is said to have been the first native-born author of the province of New York. This young girl at the age of sixteen went from the wild-beast-ridden, Indian-haunted wilds of the west, in the province of New York, to the gay metropolis of London. Here she was much courted and fêted. Among her admirers were Smollet, Fielding, Richardson, and Doctor Johnson—the latter wrote epilogues and prologues for her plays, championed her novels and poems, and made her the fashion of the hour. From this eighteenth century beginning we may trace the evolution of American fiction through the writers of the sentimental school, Mrs. Ellett, Mrs. Embury, and Mrs. Pindah; through the works of Caroline Cheseboro, Mrs. Kirkland, and the earlier writings of Grace Greenwood, to the novel which portrays the manners of our own day—the pleasing, graceful stories of Amelia Barr, Grace Litchfield, Mary Hallock Foote; the society studies of Mrs. Burton Harrison and Mrs. Van Rensselaer Cruger, and the character studies and sketches of Augusta Larned and Maria Louisa Pool. There are eighty-one volumes of children's serials; conspicuous among them are those of Mary Mapes Dodge, "who," Mrs. Thompson says, in her Wednesday Afternoon Club report, "slid into celebrity upon the silver skates of 'Hans Brinker.'" and who has been long and honorably known as

CARVED WOOD PANEL. UNITED STATES.

the editor of *St. Nicholas.* Many valuable books command attention in the department of the "Miscellanies." Notable among these are "Musical Instruments and Their Homes," by Mrs. Julia Crosby Brown; a very complete collection of the works of Miss Catherine Beecher; a "History of French Painting," by Mrs. J. S. T. Stranahan, and thirty-one volumes by Lydia Maria Child. It is of interest to note that one of the few Afro-Americans connected with the World's Fair, in an official way, is a member of the New York State Board of Women Managers, who volunteered to collect the works of Mrs. Child as a tribute from the blacks to her noble work in the anti-slavery cause. A very interesting department is made up of books written by New York women in foreign tongues. Among these there are "The Acts of the Apostles," in Burmese, by Mrs. Judson; the "Standard Dictionary of the Swatow Dialect,"

"The Life of Christ," and a volume of translations of some of the most familiar English hymns, in this dialect, by Miss Adele Field; "The Peep of Day," in Arabic, by Ellen Jackson Foote; "Early Church History" and "Legends of Helena, and Monica the Mother of St. Augustine," in Hindustani, by Mrs. Humphrey; a number of books written in German by Talvi (Mrs. Edward Robinson)—many of these have great literary and historical value; and one translation from English into French, entitled "Dans un Phare." In scientific literature we have an especially valuable collection of medical works by the women doctors of the State, while in the 219 volumes of original verse, many well-known songs and lyrics are to be found. Conspicuous among these are "Rocked in the Cradle of the Deep," by Mrs. Anna Willard; "Rock Me to Sleep, Mother," by Mrs. Elizabeth Akers Allen; "One Sweetly Solemn Thought," by Phœbe Carey; "I Love to Steal Awhile Away," by Mrs. Francis Brown; and last and best known, the famous lyric, "The Battle Hymn of the Republic," by Mrs. Julia Ward Howe. In history we have the "Standard Colonial History of New York," by Mrs. Martha J. Lamb; the "History of Woman Suffrage," by Susan B. Anthony, and the "Sabbath in Puritan New England," by Mrs. Alice Morse Earle.

These books, with many others of great value and interest, form only the first part of the New York exhibit. The second part consists of a showing of the work of seventy-five literary clubs and classes in the State. These records are type-written, and beautifully bound in leather covers bearing the seal of the State. Each volume contains the constitution, by-laws, list of members, and history of the club, with four representative papers, written by its members. These hang upon a standard at one extremity of the bookshelves. These records have been collected and installed by Sorosis, which has served as a sub-

BOOK COVER.
BOSTON
COLLECTION.
UNITED STATES.

committee for the Board of Women Managers. Another standard holds thirty-nine folios, bound like the club folios, except that the seal is white instead of blue. On these two posts there are practically four exhibits in one. Two of the folios contain a list of 3,000 names of the women of the State who have contributed to the press, while a third volume holds a list of editors and assistant editors. These records have been prepared by the Buffalo Graduates Club, to show the important part New York women take in periodical literature. A literary

council was formed, with Mrs. Runkle as chairman. The field of periodical literature was analyzed and divided into its most conspicuous departments. A woman who is an authority in each of these lines of work was asked to make a collection of the most brilliant articles written by New York women on these various subjects, the collections being as far as possible chronological. There are thirty-four of these little volumes, each a charming and interesting book in itself. Messrs. Harper & Bros. are about to publish six of these folios in book form, under the title "The Distaff Series." The thirty-nine folios which hang upon this post are also an exhibit of model type-writing. This work, done by Miss Louise Conklin of New York, with expert assistants, is a most beautiful illustration of the fact that any craft may become an art through the perfection of its execution. This work has been prepared by

OIL PAINTING—LANDSCAPE. FRAU SCHROEDER. GERMANY.

the Board of Women Managers of the State of New York, in the hope that it may prove an ornament to the woman's library, which is the gift of their State to the Woman's Building, and that it may permanently benefit working-women, for whose labor in many directions it fixes a standard.

BLANCHE WILDER BELLAMY.

Engraved by Rand, McNally & Co.

THE NORTHERN PAVILION OF HORTICULTURAL BUILDING AND EXHIBIT OF HOT-HOUSES AND SUMMER-HOUSES.

PANEL—"INFLUENCE OF WOMAN IN THE ARTS. SHE WEEPS WITH THE POET, CONSOLES HIM, AND GLORIFIES HIM." FRANCE.

PANEL—"THE ARTS OF WOMAN· TO LOVE, TO PLEASE, AND DEVOTE HERSELF." FRANCE.

Engraved by Rand, McNally & Co.

CENTRAL PORTION OF THE HORTICULTURAL BUILDING.

DOME, 114 FEET IN HEIGHT; 180 FEET IN DIAMETER. ARCHITECTS, MESSRS. W. L. B. JENNEY AND W. B. MUNDIE.

EVOLUTION OF WOMEN'S EDUCATION IN THE UNITED STATES.

WHILE the people of Massachusetts were still living in log huts, the school had its separate home, and as early as 1642 the selectmen of every town were "required to have a vigilant eye over their brethren and neighbors, to see that none of them shall suffer so much barbarism in their families as not to endeavor to teach, by themselves or others, their children and apprentices so much learning as may enable them to read the English tongue and obtain a knowledge of the capital laws, upon penalty of twenty shillings for each neglect therein," and one man must be spared from the plow and the gun, "to teach, in every township whose number had increased to fifty households." This led to the district school, which served the early scattering communities well, but was a hindrance at a later period.

The principle that the education of the people is the safeguard of the State *was at once recognized, and also the right of the State to compel the attention of parents to it.* Religious and industrial instruction were provided for, and thus the great questions which are now taking the lead in our country were anticipated in the beginning by those whom Macaulay calls "the men illustrious forever in history, the founders of the Commonwealth of Massachusetts."

And equally with the firm foundation for rudimentary instruction, the higher education was kept in mind, and provision made for the high or Latin school, leading up to the university.

But, provident as our fathers were, they did not foresee the part which women were to take in the future life of the Republic, and failed to provide for their public education on the same broad basis as that of men. And yet Mary Dyer and Anne Hutchinson introduced the woman question into the councils of the colony, and so opened it that it has been kept open till this hour, when it is still awaiting an answer from the justice of the State.

But while the colony made little provision for the education of women, yet, as many of them came from the best class in England, much attention was paid to the private instruction of the daughters of good families. Anne Dudley Bradstreet published a volume of poems in 1650, although she records in her verse the opposition made to her literary occupation.

The public schools established in 1635 made small provision for women, and even in 1789, when both sexes were to be admitted, the

SKETCH FOR WINDOW. A. F. NORTHROP. UNITED STATES.

girls could only attend from April to October. The rule which was adopted, "that no children under seven years should be received in the schools," proved advantageous to women, for, as many thought instruction needful for children at an earlier age, Sunday-schools added secular instruction to their religious work,

and as these schools were under the care of female teachers, a body
of experienced women were ready to take charge of the primary
schools when they were established, thus introducing the employment of women as teachers, which forms so marked a feature in
our schools.   The charity schools also helped to correct the

ENAMELED CUP—"THE FOUR SEASONS." MARIE LOUVET. FRANCE.

inequality in the education of boys and girls, as they were in most
instances established by ladies for girls only.

While speaking of primary education I should mention its last
development in the "Kindergarten," which was begun in Boston,
from whence it has spread over the country.   Miss Elizabeth P.
Peabody, whose life has been devoted to education, first introduced
Froebel's system into this country by a small kindergarten, established in Boston in 1861.   Mrs. Pauline Agassiz Shaw established
and supported for fifteen years sixteen free kindergartens, which

she eventually presented, fully equipped, to the city of Boston. Mrs. Shaw has initiated and carried on, at her own expense and under her active supervision, experiments and instruction in

COSTUME OF A YOUNG GIRL OF THE ISLE OF AMAGER. DENMARK.

manual training for public-school children, normal classes in kindergarten, and manual training for teachers, as well as industrial schools, vacation schools, and day-nurseries for the poor children in the crowded districts of Boston. She is now supplementing this work by liberal university-extension plans for the benefit of the same localities. Mrs. Shaw's private preparatory school for boys

SCREEN—DESIGN IN NATIONAL STYLE. K. PETRE. SWEDEN.

and girls holds a unique position among educational institutions. In the course of study pursued, the natural sciences and their co-relation with all other branches of education hold an important place. The value of Mrs. Shaw's work can hardly be overestimated, it is so far-reaching in its wisdom and its influence. Miss Blow has done a similar work for St. Louis and the West.

The "grammar schools" have always furnished the most important part of instruction to the mass of people in Massachusetts. They were open to girls, but under varying conditions. The question of co-education of the sexes was differently settled, according to the prejudices of school boards or the local condition of the school.

At the present time great differences in this respect may be found. In some towns all the schools are alike open to both sexes; in others the two unite in the primary school, are separated in the grammar schools, and come together again in the high school. The high schools are generally open to both sexes, except in the old part of Boston, where ancient prejudice leads to the duplication of the high and Latin schools, and in some towns where an endowed school for girls was already in existence.

While the public schools were thus progressing, both in their methods of work and their relation to women, it would be unfair not to recognize the service done by many large private schools and academies, some of which have retained public confidence for many years, advancing with the demands of the times. Without detracting from the merits of others, I would specially name the Mt. Holyoke Seminary, founded by Mary Lyon in the western part of the State. This was originally established in the interest of the (so called) Evangelical churches, and its object was understood to be to train women for mission life, as the wives of missionaries going out to foreign service.

But, however much this purpose narrowed the scope of instruction in its earlier days, the institution has broadened and liberalized until now it has lately received the charter of a college, and its graduates are often highly accomplished in branches not specially adapted to work among the heathens.

Its original plan, like that of Wellesley College, contemplated the union of industrial labor with study, and so made a valuable contribution toward the discussion of the question now so prominent—industrial education. The academies generally admitted both sexes, and thus naturally solved the question of co-education.

President Eliot once gave it as his opinion that the improvement of these endowed academies was the best method of giving women all the higher education they needed. But there was a dangerous tendency in them to desultory work and a want of

HANGINGS EMBROIDERED IN THE SCHOOL OF MME. LUCE BEN-ABEN.
MOORISH GIRLS AND WOMEN OF ALGIERS.

definite aim, either in preparation for a profession or in fitting for a college education, which made them less valuable to women than the public schools.

In the larger towns and cities were many private schools of more or less excellence, and they are still improving in their methods and doing much good work, although I agree with the opinion expressed by a foreign educator who came to study our schools, that the best of them are not equal in scope and thoroughness to our public schools.

The next important step was much more practical than the establishment of academies, and was directly under the control of the State. Already in New York normal teaching had been established by appropriating the excess of the annual revenue of the Library Fund to the academies for this purpose. On March 12, 1838, Horace Mann reported to the Massachusetts Legislature that "private munificence had placed conditionally at his disposal the sum of $10,000, to be disbursed under the Board of Education in qualifying teachers of our public schools." The question at once arose, "Should the board establish special schools, or attempt to engraft the department for the qualification of teachers upon the existing academies?" Mr. Mann opposed the latter plan, as the new department would be a secondary interest in the academy, and added: "The course of studies commonly pursued at the academies consists rather in an extension of knowledge into the higher departments of science than in reviewing and thoroughly and critically mastering the rudiments or elementary branches of knowledge." Still more, Mr. Mann maintains the superiority of the female teacher over the male in instructing young children, and claims that the board had acted wisely "in appropriating their first normal school exclusively to the qualification of female teachers," a proof of his belief "in the relative efficiency of the female sex in the ministry of civilization." The result of these institutions is seen in the improvement of the schools of Massachusetts, and the employment of the large force of women as teachers. The first normal school for women was established at Lexington, in 1839.

In Massachusetts 76 per cent of the teachers employed in the public schools were women as early as 1858, and the enrollment of women in the normal schools for the last thirteen years has varied from 83 to 95 per cent. The willingness of women to work for less pay than men has contributed to their employment, but even when chosen from this motive, the work has proved so satisfactory as to lead to consideration of the question of equal wages for equal work.

As yet there appears no very encouraging improvement in the salary of the average teacher, which about equals that of a weaver in a cotton mill, yet as women are advanced to higher positions,

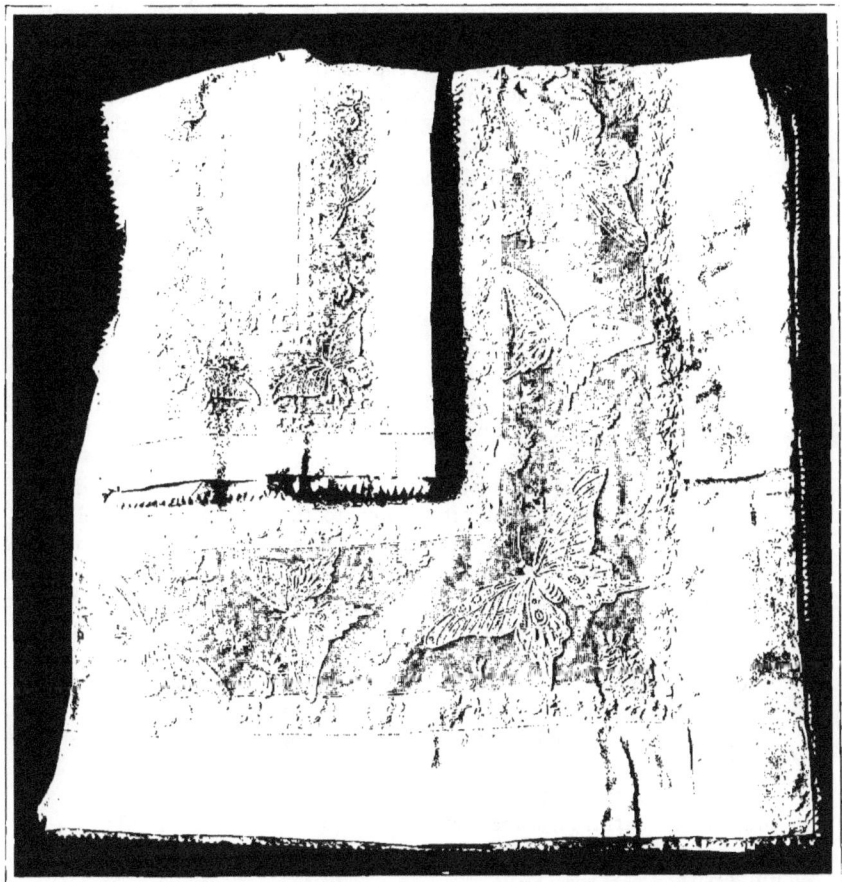

SPREAD AND PILLOW COVER. M. CROUVEZIER. FRANCE.

and salaries are increased in proportion to length of service, there are some teachers sufficiently paid to encourage the devotion of the best talent to this service.

The result of the normal teaching is well expressed in the 47th

Massachusetts Report: "The returns prove what reason would predict, that there is the same difference between trained and untrained teachers as in all other occupations and professions."

While established mainly to provide competent teachers, the normal system has benefited women by introducing them into an admirable field of employment with special training. It used to be a current saying: "If a father dies, the daughter goes to the normal school." The lesson of preparation was sadly needed by women. Education as a training for a distinct calling was almost unknown among them. They were supposed to kn w "by intuition," and they gained such knowledge as became necessary in practical life in a hap-hazard way, going mostly to the hard school of Experience, whose lessons are indeed valuable, but often purchased at a terrible price. The great business of housekeeping was committed to women, but no training in chemistry or sanitary laws, or economy of food or fuel, was considered necessary to prepare her for the work.

She was the nurse of the sick, and often, in early days, the midwife and doctor, but she was only furnished with a rude mass of traditional or empirical knowledge, which had no basis in scientific reasoning.

She only knew of law by feeling its hand heavy upon her, and, like Anne Hutchinson, found it perilous to think freely for herself in matters of religion. Even in artistic pursuits the idea of training had hardly entered her mind. It was indeed necessary to spend many hours at the piano to accomplish playing the "Battle of Prague" with the necessary dash, but nobody dreamed of any acquaintance with the science of music; and as regards drawing, when the School of Design for women was opened in 1851, the young applicants were appalled on learning that six months' training would be required before they could hope for remunerative employment.

But one step leads to another, and having once tasted the delights of learning, women were not content with the academy and high school, when they saw their brothers going to the university.

Two important colleges for women, Wellesley and Smith, have been endowed by private gifts. They are both flourishing and doing good service; but of greater moment was the opening of Boston University in 1871, which gives to women equal opportunity with men in all departments, and the opening of the Institute of Technology to women on perfectly equal terms with men.

OIL PAINTING—"MOLLY'S BALL DRESS." KATE PERUGINI. ENGLAND.

These institutions are quietly carrying on their work, and educating many women for teaching and professional life. Tufts College has followed their good example.

The Harvard Annex, as it is usually called, is a somewhat anomalous institution, having no connection with the university of that name, except that its professors, at their own pleasure, give lectures to the students. It is not a regular college conferring degrees, but its standard is high, its instruction good, and it is thus helping the higher education of women. I hope it will soon lead our most venerable university, for whose good name we are naturally jealous, to open its doors to the women of Massachusetts, who have done so much for it in the past and the present time.

The opening of Boston University in all its branches has superseded the necessity of separate schools for women in law and medicine. Its medical school is very flourishing, but it is greatly to be hoped that the Harvard Medical School will soon admit women, as the Massachusetts Medical Society has already done. The training schools for nurses are rapidly increasing, and the New England Hospital gives opportunity for clinical study.

In plastic art and music the way is freely opened by many admirable schools.

The introduction of the teaching of cooking, sewing, and gymnastic instruction into the public schools, which was accomplished through the private beneficence of Mrs. Mary Hemenway, and of sanitary chemistry in the Institute of Technology, are leading up to a genuine training for the important business of household management, which should take its place among honorable and remunerative occupations. A club within the Association of Collegiate Alumnæ has made a special study of this subject, doing admirable work in it. Mrs. Hemenway is a citizen whom Boston delights to honor. Besides the great outlay of time, energy, and capital made in the industrial improvement of our school system, she has for several years supported a course of free lectures on American history, at the Old South Church, and has founded and supported several educational institutions in the Southern States.

An important object-lesson in the political education of women is furnished by the attainment of suffrage in the choice of school committees, the appointment in a single year of some hundred and fifty women to this office in Massachusetts, and the election of women as supervisors, superintendents, and on the Board of Education. This reform is rapidly spreading throughout many States.

It being impossible to treat the question of woman's education

EASTERN FAÇADE OF THE ELECTRICITY BUILDING.

DOME OF THE ILLINOIS BUILDING IN THE DISTANCE. VIEWED FROM THE MAIN BASIN.

THE FISHERIES BUILDING.

EXTREME LENGTH, 1,100 FEET; WIDTH, 200 FEET. ARCHITECT, MR. HENRY I. COBB. COST, $225,000.

Engraved by Rand, McNally & Co.

throughout the country in the brief space allowed, I have given the story of its development in Massachusetts as enabling me to present it in a more clear and connected form, and also because the roots of the whole system were planted in this colony, which was more truly representative of the future America perhaps than any other.

But the march of education, as of empire, "westward takes it way," and since the opening of the great regions west of the Alleghanies to settlement, the school-house and the school-book—normal school, college, kindergarten, and training school—have gone with the emigrants over the mountains, and like the plants of other climes found congenial soil and grown more vigorously, but they have left behind them many enemies and parasites that checked their growth in their native regions. Especially has the education of women thus prospered. Co-education of the sexes has found less prejudice to contend with in the West than in the East. The noble stand taken by the University of Michigan, founded in 1837, in opening its doors freely to women, instead of hindering its prosperity, has helped to place it among the four oldest and best colleges of the country in rank.

Yale College, in Connecticut, one of the most conservative institutions in the country, has lately taken the last step first and invited women to her post-graduate courses. So many other institutions have fallen into this line of progress, that now it has been said by a superintendent of education that "a college course is looked upon as the rational and proper method of fitting a girl to do her share in the work of the world."

To carry out this last idea, the alumnæ of colleges admitting women have formed an association throughout the country to promote education. It numbers 1,458 members, of whom 175 have received master's or doctor's degrees, and 31 fellowship; 55 of the members are married women. They have done much to promote many practical measures, and have formed a bureau for the employment of teachers, which has led to a demand for college training for the teachers of all higher schools. It is significant, however, that while the highest salary for a non-resident teacher has been only $1,400, "the best situation has been offered by an insurance company for a private secretary of high attainments in stenography and higher mathematics."

The normal school system has also been extended over the whole Union. There are some twenty-three thousand pupils in the schools of thirty-eight States, and 71 per cent of them are women.

11

In the commercial colleges, even, nearly one-third of the pupils are of the female sex, while in the training schools for nurses, now rapidly multiplying, the preponderance is, of course, the other way, as in 33 schools there are 956 women to 76 men.

COPY OF WATTEAU SCREEN, LOUIS XV. DESIGN, AT THE TUILERIES.
WORKED BY THE COUNTESS TANKERVILLE. ENGLAND.

The same rapid and extensive development is seen in the establishment of manual training schools, so that it is difficult to give full statistics; but, while the men appear to outnumber women twelve to one, yet a very important opportunity is thus opened to both sexes. This work has proved admirably adapted to the colored schools of the South, which have been such an important feature in American education for the last thirty years. It has enabled the students to pay in part for their tuition, as well as to undertake varied occupation on leaving school. Its excellent moral effect has also been noted. The branches taught are very numerous, from iron and wood work, brick-making, etc., to cooking, sewing, and fancy carving. The Le Moyne Institute has adopted the sensible plan of teaching the boys cooking and sewing and the girls carpentry work in addition to their other lessons.

One other general feature must be named — the advance in supplementing by education the deficiency in the usual five senses. The fame of Laura Bridgman's development is far-spread, and from that wonderful experiment a course of training has been established by which the blind almost see, and the deaf and dumb speak and hear, at least so much as secures the development of their intelligence and the ability to lead happy and useful lives. Women have taken a large share in this work.

DESIGN FOR HAND MIRROR.
Mrs. E. W. BLASHFIELD. UNITED STATES.

It is a trite saying that "a republic must be based on general education." This slight survey will show how much has been and is doing to lay this foundation broad and deep, and how essential it is that women, to whom education is so largely intrusted, not only in schools but in the far more important training of the home and every-day life, should have every opportunity freely opened to them.

Thus clearly has the evolution of education been progressing from the earliest settlement of the country until the present moment. A few gaps remain to be filled before women can go on with equal pace with men. The great law of the survival of the fittest will insure that —

> "What is excellent,
> As God lives, is permanent."

EDNA D. CHENEY.

DESIGN FOR BANNER. Miss Digby, England.

MUSIC IN THE WOMAN'S BUILDING.

FINDING myself appointed chairman of the Committee on Music in the Woman's Building, by Mrs. Potter Palmer, and feeling somewhat overcome at the immense and unexplored field for work that lay before me, it occurred to me that here also might lie the same opportunity for "helping women to help themselves" that has been the underlying motive of all the woman's work of the Columbian Exposition; therefore I submitted, with some hesitation, a little plan for securing amateur music in the Woman's Building to Mr. Theodore Thomas, Musical Director-General. Mr. Thomas found something worthy in the idea, and indorsed my plan heartily, lending me his advice and coöperation, which have proved of inestimable value. After studying the possibilities which lay in my original idea, that of affording a hearing in the Woman's Building for amateurs of distinction, I sent the following circular to all the Lady Managers, asking their sympathy and assistance in their various States:

"Believing that the progress of American women in musical knowledge and experience can not be more simply and effectively shown, the National Committee on Music in the Woman's Building at the Exposition has designed a series of musical illustrations after the following plan, briefly outlined: It is proposed to give semi-monthly concerts in the Woman's Building at Chicago during the six months of the Exposition, at which only women or girls who are amateurs, possessed of talent and a high order of musical ability, and who have been residents of America for at least ten years, will be permitted to appear. The qualifications of any one desiring to take part must first be tested and approved by a jury selected by the Woman's National Committee on Music, and satisfactory to Theodore Thomas, Musical Director of the Exposition. No musical prodigy will be admitted simply as such, nor is the diploma of any college or conservatory either necessary or sufficient. Each candidate will be rated upon her merits, technical proficiency not alone being considered. Permission to appear at

MOORISH WOMAN PREPARING COUSCOUSSON. ALGERIA.

these concerts will be a mark of high honor, and will confer a lasting distinction, the advantages of which can not be overestimated.

"Minnesota has decided to bestow a medal upon each successful candidate belonging to that State, and it is hoped that other States will follow its example. The concerts are intended to provide a public appearance for those amateurs of distinction who are shut out from the concert-room of the professional, and who, for various reasons, may not wish to appear therein. Quartettes, trios, either vocal or instrumental, choral and orchestral organizations of women will be eligible for examination. The examinations will take place not later than February, 1893, either at Chicago or at several cities in the different States. It is hoped that all candidates for these concerts will communicate with the chairman of the Woman's Board for their State, or with the undersigned, as soon as possible. It is also desired that all women following music as a profession, and wishing to appear in the Woman's Building, will

FRENCH COLBERT POINT LACE FLOUNCE.
EXHIBITED BY LEFEBURE. FRANCE.

make application to Theodore Thomas, Musical Director of the Exposition.

"The National Committee on Music in the Woman's Building congratulates itself that in the above plan it has the hearty sympathy of Theodore Thomas and of the entire Bureau of Music, and that it finds itself in complete harmony with the broader and more comprehensive scheme of musical illustration as outlined by Mr. Thomas in his first official bulletin, recently issued. It needs but a cordial response and earnest effort on the part of American women to win for their sex such a recognition as the great occasion alone makes possible."

EMBROIDERED LINEN TOILET TABLE, DRAPERY, XVII CENTURY DESIGN.
MADE AT MME. NARISCHKINE'S SCHOOL. RUSSIA.

The responses that came to me in return were many and earnest. Few States in the Union failed to appoint advisory committees and pass upon the applicants desirous of availing themselves of this opportunity of being heard in the Woman's Building. Many of these States followed the example set by Minnesota, and awarded diplomas — in one instance a gold medal — to the successful candidates.

The next step for the candidates, after passing the State examination, is to appear before the expert jury in Chicago, appointed by Mr. Thomas. This jury congratulates itself upon calling Mr. Mees of the Exposition orchestra its chairman, while the other members are the well-known musicians, Mrs. Clarence Eddy, Mrs. Bloomfeld Zeisler, and Mr. Burritt.

Owing to the unavoidable delays attendant upon such matters, the first examination by the final jury will not take place until June the 13th, the first concert on June the 15th. If the "médaille d'honneur" to be awarded each successful candidate by Mr. Thomas' expert jury and the National Committee on Music, of which I have the honor to be chairman, prove a steppingstone toward a larger sphere of usefulness, or a possible means of assisting women in the honorable struggle for independence, I shall feel that

BRONZE GROUP—"BROTHER AND SISTER."
FRAULEIN FINZELBERG. GERMANY.

my work has been blessed beyond my deepest hopes.

I can not close this brief statement without expressing my sincere appreciation of the interest taken in this work by Mrs. Palmer, to whom I am deeply indebted, as are so many other women, for support and encouragement. My sincere thanks are also due to Mr. George H. Wilson of the Bureau of Music for his unfailing courtesies; and also to Mrs. Theodore Thomas, Mrs. George B. Carpenter, and Mrs. Edward Barbour for similar kindnesses.

LENA BURTON CLARKE.

EMBROIDERED SCREEN. GABRIELLE DELESSERT, NÉE DE LABORDE. FRANCE.

CONGRESSES IN THE WOMAN'S BUILDING.

THE daily introduction of one or more distinguished women of this and other countries to the large and appreciative audiences which throng our Assembly Room is found to be one of the leading attractions of the Woman's Building.

This feature was inaugurated under a resolution passed by the Board of Lady Managers providing for a committee on Congresses to be held in the Woman's Building. Mrs. Potter Palmer appointed

CARVED WOOD PANEL. ALBERTINA NORDSTROM. UNITED STATES.

the following ladies to serve on this important committee: Mrs. James P. Eagle of Arkansas, chairman, Mrs. Helen M. Barker of South Dakota, Miss Laurette Lovell of Arizona, Miss Ellen M. Russell of Nevada, Mrs. Susan R. Ashley of Colorado, Mrs. L. M. N. Stevens of Maine, and Mrs. Lewis of Illinois. Before the committee was called together it lost two valued members, Mrs. Susan R. Ashley, who resigned from the Board on account of ill health, and Mrs. Lewis by decease. Mrs. John J. Bagley of Michigan and Mrs. L. Brace Shattuck of Illinois were appointed to fill the vacancies.

Owing to the nature of the work of this committee, which required an immense amount of correspondence, the most careful keeping of records of all engagements and partial engagements, the arrangement of dates to meet the convenience of the 300 and more women who are to appear on the programme during the

OIL PAINTING—"THOUGHTS." FRAULEIN LUBBES. GERMANY.

Exposition, and the keeping up with the post office addresses of the busy throng, it was found almost impossible to divide the work by assigning certain duties to each member of the committee. At the first meeting of the committee resolutions were passed indicating the character of work desired, and instructing the chairman to proceed to fill up the programme by providing one or two gifted women to read papers or deliver addresses each day during the Exposition. When the nature of the subject permits, an opportunity for free discussion is afforded.

Every avocation, profession, department, or line of work, of whatsoever nature, that has enlisted the interest and activity of women will be offered an opportunity for presentation through their most distinguished advocates at some time during these six months of daily intellectual feasts for women.

It is a rare opportunity for persons visiting the Exposition to be brought in touch with many distinguished contemporary women of this and other countries, whose names are known throughout the civilized world, and who have consented to aid our work.

If in a different age and under other governments women have been suppressed, at the Columbian Exposition at least they are guaranteed the right of free speech under the most favorable circumstances. Such a dissemination of thought can not fail to broaden woman's sphere of usefulness and facilitate her advancement.

The golden opportunity for women has for some wise purpose been reserved to this good time, and is now placed in the hands of the women of our country, to crown the Columbian year. With united effort and singleness of purpose our Board has worked with the view of uplifting and benefiting all classes of women the world over. All the results of their labor they can not hope to see, but the children of to-day may behold it to-morrow. This department, providing for interchange of ideas and the close communion of thought, which always tends to overcome prejudice, and knit together the highest interests of humanity, will not be an unimportant factor when the grand result of the perfect whole is calculated.

MARY K. O. EAGLE.

CARVED BUFFET. COUNTESS TANKERVILLE. ENGLAND.

ASSOCIATIONS OF WOMEN.

THE parable of the mustard-seed, of the great tree that grows from the smallest beginnings, is illustrated by many facts of common experience, and nowhere more than in the history of the beginning and progress of the associations among women, which have come to play so important a part in the development of American society. Sporadic instances of women's clubs appear here and there in the history of the last fifty years, but the movement which has culminated in the General Federation of Women's Clubs may be said to have had its beginning twenty-five years ago, when, within a few weeks of each other, the New England Woman's Club of Boston and the Sorosis of New York came into being, each with a name and plan of action.

The first of these had its immediate origin in a desire to furnish some convenient place for meeting and resting to the many ladies who reside in the suburbs of Boston, and are often called to the city by various occasions of business or of pleasure. Several ladies, remarkable for sound judgment and superior culture, associated themselves in this enterprise, and established it on a practical basis. Parlors were engaged in a central part of the city, and the club was duly installed, its numbers at the first amounting to one hundred and eighteen—with seventeen associate members. The *locale* being secured, plans of utilizing it began to develop themselves, resulting in the institution of a weekly meeting for the hearing of lectures and the discussion of topics considered of importance. These exercises rapidly increased in interest and value, and the Mondays of the month—Monday being the chosen day—were entrusted to the care of various committees. The first Monday in the month belonged to the Art and Literature Committee, and was occupied by a lecture, usually by an outsider, followed by a short discussion of the topic presented. The second Monday was assigned to the Discussion Committee, and was wholly devoted to its work, which was introduced by a short paper contributed by a member of the club. The third Monday was given to the Work Committee, and at this meeting many grave topics of public interest were presented, often by experts, and commented upon. The fourth Monday, at first reserved for some popular entertainment, was at last given in charge to the Committee on Education. To these occasions was soon added a Club Tea, following the discussion of the Work Committee afternoon.

The club embraced in its membership a number of able women, and the zeal of the more thoughtful soon made itself felt through-

TAPESTRY FROM RAPHAEL'S CARTOON, "THE MIRACULOUS DRAUGHT OF FISHES." ANNIE LYMAN. UNITED STATES.

out the whole body. Questions very important to the community, and reforms which have proved very valuable, were sometimes started at these meetings, and have been much forwarded by the action of the club. While remaining distinctively a woman's club, a few eminent men were admitted to its fellowship. Prominent among these were William Lloyd Garrison, Ralph Waldo Emerson, the poet Whittier, and noble Judge Sewall, the untiring champion of the political and civil rights of women. Miss Abby W. May, a woman eminent in the community for judgment and character, was the life-long chairman of the Work Committee. Mrs. Caroline M.

Severance was the first president of the club. The writer of this paper succeeded her, and has remained in that office ever since. The secretary from the start has been Miss Lucia M. Peabody, well known in her earlier life as one of the ablest educators in New England. The club, whose membership has extended to 230, has

MINIATURE. CAMILLE ISBERT. FRANCE.

for years past occupied pleasant parlors on Park Street, a region once consecrated to highest fashion.

The methods of the New York Sorosis were somewhat different from those just described. This club chose for its place of meeting a large and convenient parlor in Delmonico's well-known restaurant, where luncheon was usually served to them. Their meetings were once a fortnight, and while sometimes devoted to the gravest questions, were often enlivened by music and recitations. The

membership is larger than that of the New England Women's
Club, the annual fee for each being ten dollars, with an initiation fee
of five dollars.   This club has a good record, having always been
active in works of charity and in social and æsthetic culture.   The
Association for the Advancement of Women, of which we shall
presently speak, was first planned by members of Sorosis, and the
general federation of women's clubs, which is now so prominent
in the country, was also devised by it, a similar plan having been

ARABIAN EMBROIDERY FROM SCHOOL FOR MOORISH AND ALGERIAN GIRLS.
EXHIBITED BY MME. LUCE BEN-ABEN, ALGERIA.

suggested in the New England Women's Club, but not carried into
action.
    The Fortnightly Club and the Woman's Club, both of Chicago,
next claim our attention.   The first of these was founded by Mrs.
Kate Newell Doggett, a woman of much intelligence, energy, and
cultivation.   Being herself a sedulous student of foreign literature,
of botany, and sociology, she made every effort to inspire the ladies
of her city with a love for the same high pursuits.   The Fort-
nightly has always been purely literary in character, and has done

much to improve the tone and taste of Chicago society. The Woman's Club, instituted by Mrs. Caroline N. Brown some years later, has had a more varied scope, including in its interests reform and humanitarian action. To this club is owing the appointment

PORTRAIT OF PRINCE BARIATINSKY. PRINCESS OLGA BARIATINSKY. RUSSIA.

of matrons on the Chicago police force, a measure which has been attended with very good results. Each of these clubs has had, until lately, a parlor of its own, and as these were in the same building, each could sometimes enjoy the advantages of both rooms. I will

CARVED FAN. COUNTESS TANKERVILLE. ENGLAND.

only further say that both clubs are now in active and successful operation.

The Association for the Advancement of Women, familiarly spoken of as the A. A. W., was instituted by the New York Sorosis in 1873. Mrs. Jenny June Croly had, at an earlier period, issued a call for a congress of women, which resulted in the holding of a parliamentary conference in the city of New York. No organization, however, resulted from this. At the date given above a call was issued to women of many pursuits and occupations, some of them already known by reputation. This was signed by the president of Sorosis, and other officers. The first congress was held in New York, and was largely attended. Mrs. Livermore was its president; Mrs. Charlotte B. Wilbour, then president of Sorosis, was chairman of the executive committee. The meetings lasted for three days, and the papers and discussions received very favorable notice in the public prints. Conspicuous among those who attended it were Mrs. Elizabeth Cady Stanton, Mrs. Isabella Beecher Hooker, Mrs. Sara Spencer of Washington, D. C., Antoinette Brown Blackwell, and Maria Mitchell, professor of astronomy at Vassar college, and the writer. Miss Alice C. Fletcher, now so well known as a student of ethnology and as a friend to the Indians, was the efficient and valued secretary of the association. This congress resulted in the formation of a permanent association, whose office it became to hold a yearly congress in various important cities of the Union, with a special view to the instruction of their own sex and the formation of women's clubs, many of which resulted from its influence. The plan of the Association was rather vague at first, but the labor bestowed upon it resulted in the formation of various committees, among which its work was divided. Its second president was Maria Mitchell, who served in that capacity with great acceptance for two years. She was succeeded by Mrs. Doggett of Chicago, who in turn was followed by Mrs. Julia Ward Howe, who still remains president of the association. The congresses have been held in Boston, Providence, Portland (Me.), Syracuse, Buffalo, Grand Rapids, Denver, Toronto, Baltimore, Cleveland, Louisville, Memphis, and other cities, and in all of these places have awakened great interest and have stimulated association among women.

The two parent clubs, the Sorosis and the New England Women's Club, were soon consulted by various bodies of women desiring to form similar associations. To these all possible help and encouragement was given by the New England Club, and, presumably, by its sister Sorosis, and far and wide throughout the land the club movement grew and the circles multiplied. These bodies were very various in their plans and pursuits, but all were determined to do good work, and their record has been such as to win a place in the public esteem for what was at first considered a dangerous and man-aping innovation. The word *club*, indeed, is susceptible of more than one interpretation, and to many, no doubt, may have at first suggested the thought of careless manners and of idle conversation. At one of the recent woman's congresses a speaker playfully asked whether men at their clubs occupied themselves in discussing the proper ordering of their households, the education of their children, and kindred subjects. The question called forth some laughter from the audience, who were well aware that, while these topics receive much attention in women's clubs, they are not prominently brought forward in those frequented by men.

An important era in club history was marked by the institution of a general federation of women's clubs, which, like the A. A. W., was first called for by the New York Sorosis, and has now become an important factor in the community. The first president of the federation was Mrs. Charlotte Emerson Brown of Orange, N. J. This lady proved eminently qualified for the position to which she was called, having devoted much time and labor to the affairs of the federation, and having shown in her work a truly catholic and disinterested spirit. At the close of her first term of office she was reëlected with almost entire unanimity. She reports the number of clubs in the federation as over three hundred. The conventions of this body are biennial, the first having been held in New York and the second in Chicago.

This general union is likely to be supplemented by State federations, which may hold State conventions. This plan is not yet perfected.

The associations for study, and those devoted to benevolent action connected with churches of all denominations, can not be here enumerated. Among them, however, we may mention as being of especial interest, the Zenana Missions in India, instituted and supported by these associations. The Society for the Encouragement of Studies at Home, although in no sense a club, should yet be mentioned with honor among the associations of women. Its work is done by correspondence, and its years already number twenty. The following quotation from an authorized statement gives us in brief some of its features:

"In all, more than six thousand women appear on the rolls, geographically distributed over forty-three States, one Territory, and Canada.

"The methods include regular correspondence, memory notes, monthly reports of work done, frequent examinations on books or subjects—answered on honor—arranged to help the student to order and make truly hers the newly acquired knowledge; and abstracts

SILK AND GOLD EMBROIDERED PANEL.
WORKING WOMAN'S SOCIETY OF VIENNA. AUSTRIA.

of books, or papers on special points, required according to the ability of the student.

"In the seventeen years of the society's life nearly all grades of social position have been represented by our students—women of leisure, many of whom soon became helpers in the work; teachers, including a colored one in the South; graduates of colleges, some studying for a second degree; a telegraph operator, a compositor, a matron of a public institution, women from towns, and others from remote places, one of whom writes: ' With my lesson, copied at night, pinned to the kitchen wall, I find the drudgery of dishwashing removed.' "

The Women's Press Clubs are a novel feature, and should be mentioned with commendation. Their members are generally too closely occupied to partake very largely of the enjoyments of club life. Their meetings, however, are pleasant and instructive, and have done much to improve the tone of women's contributions to the press. These associations exist in Boston, Chicago, New York, and many other places.

The writer remembers the days in which a single woman reporter would shyly creep into place among half a dozen or more of the other sex. Matters are very much changed in this respect, and the group of bright young faces at the reporters' table, bearing the marks of thought and education, is now a happy feature at many public meetings.

In the Woman's Building in Chicago many associations are represented in addition to those already spoken of. The Women's Christian Temperance Union has now a world-wide reputation and efficiency. The various suffrage associations occupy space and will hold meetings from time to time.

The associations of women in these days are so numerous that we may say their name is legion, and while we salute them all with esteem and good will, we should find it impossible within our present limits to give them fuller characterization or to do more than very partial justice to their merits.

JULIA WARD HOWE.

LIST OF ORGANIZATIONS GRANTED SPACE IN THE WOMAN'S BUILDING.

Ladies' Catholic Benevolent Association	Syracuse, N. Y.
King's Daughters	New York City.
Association for Advancement of Women .	241 Beacon Street, Boston.
National Council of Women	Indianapolis, Ind.
National W. C. T. U.	New York City.
Non-Partisan W. C. T. U.	Washington, D. C.
Promotion of Physical Culture	Chicago, Ill.
Emma Willard Association	New York City.
Woman's Relief Corps	Sabetha, Kan.
International Committee of Y. W. C. A. . . .	Chicago, Ill.

Association of Collegiate Alumnæ	Washington, D. C.
Shut-in Society	Millersville, Pa.
P. E. O. Sisterhood	Nelson, Neb.
Federation of Clubs	Orange, N. J.
Woman's Columbia Club	Wichita, Kan.
American Society of Authors	Brooklyn, N. Y.
Woman's Educational Industrial Association	Boston.
Home of the Merciful Savior for Crippled Children	Philadelphia, Pa.
Chicago Woman's Club	Chicago, Ill.
Columbian Association of Housekeepers	Chicago, Ill.
National Science Club	Oberlin, Ohio.
International Woman's Christian Association	St. Louis, Mo.
New York Association of Working Girls	New York.
Stanton Woman's Relief Corps	Stanton, Cal.
South End Flower Mission	Chicago, Ill.
National Deaconesses, Conference	Chicago, Ill.
Woman's Branch Congress Auxiliary	Chicago, Ill.
Ladies' Hermitage Association	Nashville, Tenn.
Eastern Star	Chicago, Ill.
Nebraska Ceramic Club	Omaha, Neb.
The Needlework Guild	New York City.
Monticello Seminary	Godfrey, Ill.
Girls' Mutual Benefit Club	Chicago, Ill.
Mary Washington Monument Association	Chicago, Ill.
Woman's Board of Missions (Congregational)	Boston, Mass.
Woman's Board of the Interior	Chicago, Ill.
Woman's Presbyterian Board of Missions	Chicago, Ill.
Woman's National Press Federation	Washington, D. C.
Woman's Home Missionary (M. E.)	Evanston, Ill.
Woman's Foreign Missionary (M. E.)	Evanston, Ill.
L'Union des Femmes de France	Paris, France.
Woman's Work for Women	Chicago, Ill.
Girls' Friendly Society	New York, N. Y.
National Press League	Chicago, Ill.
Woman's Club of Wisconsin	Milwaukee, Wis.
Woman's National Indian Association	Philadelphia, Pa.

EDUCATIONAL.

Alumnæ Pratt Institute	Brooklyn.
Bryn Mawr School	Baltimore.
American College for Girls	Turkey.
School of Applied Arts	New York.
Technical School of Design	New York.
Lasell Seminary	Auburndale, Mass.
Helmuth College	London, Ontario.
Industrial College of Mississippi	Columbus, Miss.

Engraved by Rand, McNally & Co.   THE CONVENT OF SANTA MARIA DE LA RABIDA.   THE KRUPP, DAIRY, AND FORESTRY BUILDINGS BEYOND.

PORTRAIT OF A CHILD. ALICE GRANT. ENGLAND.

Engraved by Rand, McNally & Co.

CONVENT OF LA RABIDA, WHERE COLUMBUS WAS FED AND SHELTERED BEFORE STARTING ON HIS VOYAGE.

THE CHILDREN'S BUILDING.

THERE are certain departments of the Fair whose interest is rather special than general; there are others (and these far outnumber the former) which have a universal interest. Foremost among these stands the Children's Building. There may be a few misanthropes of both sexes among our visitors who will declare themselves indifferent to what women are doing in the world, but I believe there is no man or woman who visits the Fair who will not be glad to peep into the children's house. There are some crusty old bachelors and a few childless women who make a pretense of disliking children, but it's a flimsy sort of sour-grape antipathy, and rarely rings true. Even those people who do not like children's society will find a great deal to enjoy in their domicile. The sternest bachelor was a boy once, and he will have a sort of retrospective enjoyment of our great play-house in conjuring up his own youthful image swinging from the rings, leaping over the horses, and exercising on the parallel bars of our gymnasium. All the world loves a lover, all the world loves a child. Many of us *fear* children, and with reason; their bright eyes, their unsophisticated judgments, make them keen and wholesome critics of their elders' actions. But we love them for two reasons. They recall life's morning, when tears, and smiles, and passions were quickly roused and quickly banished; when the world was a great treasure-house, and the years were eagerly added to our span because each brought greater freedom to go out and gather the fairy gold and jewels lying in heaps before us. Childhood typifies for each of us the unsullied purity of his own soul; we love it for this, and again we love it because in the tiny hands of the infant we tend so carefully the future destiny of our race is clinched. Manhood and womanhood stand for the living present, but childhood stands for the past and for the future, and what one of us would exchange the bittersweet memories of yesterday, the dreamy visions of to-morrow, for the common-sense reality of to-day?

The Children's Building stands close to the Woman's Building, nestling under its eaves in a very natural manner. It is a pleasant

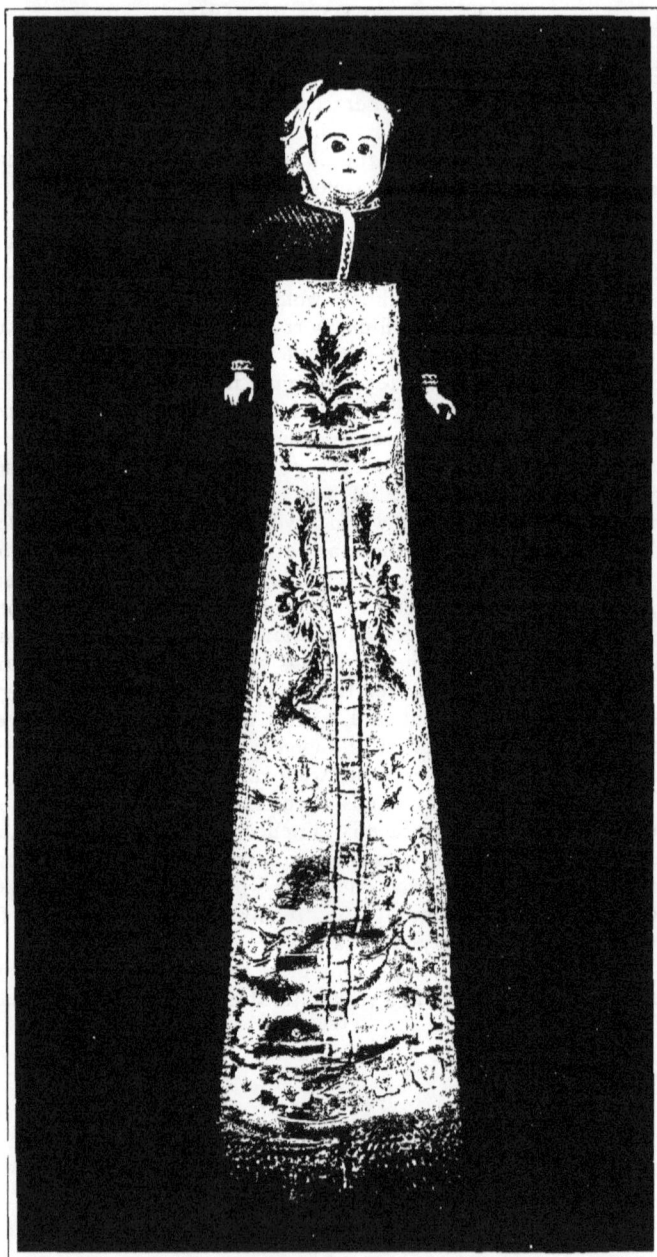

OLD BAPTISMAL GOWN. BARONESS REEDTZ THOTT, DENMARK.

two-storied edifice, with a roof garden, a large gymnasium, a library, a workshop, and all the other departments which that wonderfully complex creature, the modern child, requires for its development.

MOSES' CRADLE. MLLE. SUSSE. ANCIENNE MAISON MARINDAZ. FRANCE.

The Children's Building is intended to be, primarily, an educational exhibit. As the Transportation Building exhibits all the marvelous improvements in methods of transportation, from the cumbrous cart drawn by oxen to the palace car equipped with every luxury and convenience the genius of man can devise, so the Children's Building aims to exhibit the most improved methods

OIL PAINTING — "THE BATH."
MME. DEMONT-BRETON (DAUGHTER OF JULES BRETON). FRANCE.

adopted in the light of the nineteenth century for the rearing and education of children.

We have endeavored to make the exhibition as complete as possible, beginning with the infant at its earliest and most helpless stage. This department is in charge of Miss Maria M. Love of

Buffalo, a member of the Board of Women Managers of New York. Miss Love is carrying on a model crèche. A large, light, and airy room is devoted to the crèche. In this is demonstrated the most healthful, comfortable, and rational system of dressing and caring for young children.

Short lectures are given upon their food, clothing, and sleeping arrangements, and in connection with the crèche there is an exhibition of infants' clothing of all nations and times, their cradles, and other furniture.

As the child grows and its mental faculties develop, the kindergarten succeeds the crèche; in the gracious atmosphere of its intelligent training the child-nature expands and develops symmetrically. This department of child-life is demonstrated in the most complete manner.

The kindergarten under this management is fitted up in the most attractive manner. All the latest apparatus necessary to the best exposition of the work has been provided. Little children developing daily their intellectual and moral faculties unconsciously, by means of the most fascinating entertainments, will be an object-lesson of great practical value to mothers and others having the care of children.

Closely allied to the kindergarten is the kitchengarden. Miss Emily Huntington of New York, the founder of this system of education, conducts a kitchengarden, where classes of little folks are taught the useful arts of homekeeping. In so interesting and delightful a manner are sweeping, dusting, bedmaking, and cooking taught, that what might otherwise be an irksome task to children becomes an amusing recreation.

For older children there will be a school for slojd, supported by Mrs. Quincy Shaw, and conducted by Gustav Larsson. Here an exhibit of wood-carving may be seen.

Physical development is aptly illustrated by the North American Turner-Bund. These interesting classes will inspire many a lad to seek after that physical perfection that was the pride of the Greeks and Romans.

Mrs. Clara Doty Bates, chairman of the committee on literature for children of the Congress Auxiliary, has charge of the library, and has fitted it up tastefully, providing a full supply of children's literature. A large number of portraits of the most eminent authors of children's books adorn the walls. Here may be found the books of all lands, and in all languages, their newspapers, periodicals, etc.

13

A request sent out by the Board of Lady Managers to foreign countries, asking contributions of children's literature, met with a prompt response, and 100 volumes have been received.

The committee on literature for children of the Congress Auxiliary assumed the furnishing of the library. Its idea was—so far as books are concerned—to select the library from the child's and youth's standard, not from the point of view of the adult.

WATER-COLOR. ROSINA EMMET SHERWOOD. UNITED STATES. (Copyrighted.)

The books the children most longed for were to be upon the shelves, rather than the books their elders thought most suitable to them. To really get at an average preference in children, boys and girls of all ages were consulted and asked to send lists of their favorite books.

The matter was placed before many public and private schools, and the chairman of the committee received hundreds of letters from children, from which she expected to make up her final catalogue.

But an unexpected obstacle—indeed one so formidable that it wholly blocked the way in that direction—now appeared. It was, that the publishers had been so industriously solicited from numer-

CRADLE. WITH APPLIQUE OF MIRECOURT LACE. HAND-MADE. FRANCE.

ous other quarters that they looked upon this final straw as the one that made the burden unendurable.

They declined to send even the very modest number of books asked for. It looked as if the library would be of a novel kind— one entirely without books.

Baffled in that direction, a new plan was made. If the library could not be representative it could at least be interesting. A large number of writers for children in Europe and America were requested by personal letter each to send one book, with an autograph inside. This plan has proved most effective.

A very interesting collection of authors' copies has been made. So much for the nucleus of the library.

For its decoration we have more than a hundred portraits of

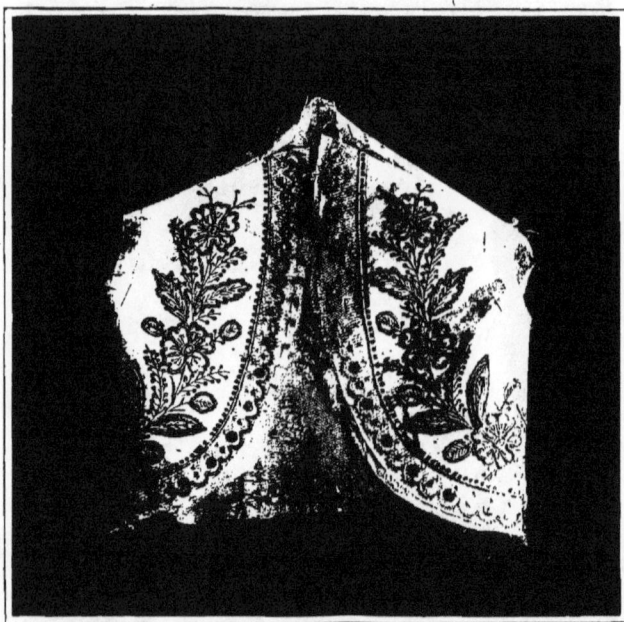

BOLERO VEST IN WHITE SATIN EMBROIDERED IN GOLD.
MME. PAILLERON. FRANCE.

writers—photographs with autographs affixed whenever possible— and prints, from the life-size to the mere cabinet.

St. Nicholas, Harper's Young People, Wide Awake, and the *Youth's Companion* make exhibits of original sketches from which their publications have been illustrated, valuable manuscripts, autographs, etc., together with the various processes by which, step by step, a complete magazine is produced.

Besides these there are interesting loans of manuscripts, artists' sketches, and photographs. One of these is a collection of views of

STATUE OF INNOCENCE. EXHIBITED BY MEXICO IN HORTICULTURAL BUILDING.

LOOKING NORTH FROM THE MINES AND MINING BUILDING.

all the haunts of Henry D. Thoreau, together with various portraits of him.

This author, while not in any sense a writer for children, is given this prominence in the house dedicated to them to attract their attention to his high pursuit of nature.

Upon the table are placed each month several copies of all the favorite children's periodicals. These are for the use of the children. A number of illustrated books have been sent, with the stipulation that children are to have them in constant service.

Pennsylvania equips and maintains a department in

EMBROIDERED PANELS.

EXHIBITED BY MME. LEROUDIER OF LYONS. FRANCE.

FAIENCE. HORTENSE RICHARD. FRANCE.

the Children's Building, showing the wonderful progress that has been made in teaching very young deaf mutes to speak. Miss Mary Garrett, secretary of the Home for Teaching Deaf Mutes to Speak, is in charge of this department. Daily demonstrations are given.

There is a department of Public Comfort in connection with the Children's Building, intended especially for the benefit of children. One hundred infants and small children are received and placed in the care of competent nurses, who, for a small fee, provide for all their wants while their mothers are visiting the various departments of the Exposition.

For the amusement of visiting children there is a large playground on the roof; this is inclosed with a strong wire netting, so the children are perfectly safe. This playground is very attractive, ornamented with vines and flowers. Here, under cover, are exhibited toys of all nations, from the rude playthings of the Esquimau children to the wonderful toys which at once instruct and amuse. These toys are used to entertain the children.

The building has an assembly-room, containing rows of little chairs, and a platform from which stereopticon lectures are given to the older boys and girls, about foreign countries, their languages, manners, and customs, and important facts connected with their history. These talks are given by kindergarteners, who then take the groups of children to see the exhibits from the countries about which they have just heard. Mr. T. H. McAllister of New York has generously given the use of the most approved stereopticon for this purpose, and the services of an operator of the same during the entire Exposition. This audience-room is also available for musical, dramatic, and literary entertainments, which will be carefully planned to suit the intelligence of children of various ages.

The Children's Building has no appropriation from the Exposition authorities. The Board of Lady Managers has assumed the responsibility of raising the money necessary for its erection.

It has been at a great outlay of time and strength that the money for the Children's Building has been raised and judiciously expended, but no one of the many workers who have contributed these precious building materials, time, and strength have grudged the costly sacrifice they have made. We believe not only that the children who enjoy our building's hospitality will be benefited by our work, but that the children in every State of the Union, in every country of the world, will directly or indirectly profit by it, and in this happy result we shall find an ample reward for what we have done.

EMMA B. DUNLAP.

PAINTING,—"FRANCE ON THE WAY TO THE CHICAGO EXPOSITION." LOUISE ABBEMA.

FRANCE.

A T the request of the managers of the International Exposition at Chicago, the French government, under date of
July 8, 1892, appointed a committee of ladies charged with
the preparation of a special woman's exhibit for the Woman's
Building. The first act of this committee was to draw up a programme and establish a general classification. But before pro-
ceeding to particulars touching the status of woman in France
and the conditions affecting her work in industrial, commercial,
and agricultural pursuits, her part in education, in the arts, the
liberal professions, and the many departments of labor wherein
foresight, sympathy, and economy are requisite, the committee
has deemed it important to show, by the aid of a certain number
of graphic charts, what is in France the true position of women
compared with that of men in the different aspects of social
life in general; that is to say, in married or single life, in the
building up of the family, vitality, etc. It is with this object
and in view, especially, of the Exposition at Chicago, that the
committee has drawn up the first statistics ever essayed of the
demographic part played by women in social economy. Thus an
important part of our general statistics has been devoted to this
entirely new study.

We have devised a series of charts, chronologically and
methodically arranged by departments and districts, in which
are shown the proportion of the two sexes in the general
population, variation in the date of marriages according to age,
locality, and the duration of married life, the number of children
therein born, the vitality, longevity, and mortality of women compared with those of men, and so on.

In another department of inquiry the part of women in emigra-
tion and immigration has been shown by a certain number of
special charts. The committee has elaborated a still more special
programme, with a view to classify the diverse economical func-
tions of women. The principal features of this programme are as
follows:

PILLOW SHAM. MME. CROUVEZIER. FRANCE.

SECTION 1.—EDUCATION. PHYSIQUE. MORALS.

Instruction: Primary, secondary, superior.

Institutions: Schools, lyceums (colleges), courses of instruction.

Grades of liberal culture open to women.

SECTION 2.

Institutions of philanthropy and social economy founded by women or depending largely upon their coöperation.

SECTION 3.

Manual labor: Industrial, commercial, administrative, and so on, for use either in home or in the workshop.

SECTION 4.—ART.

Under this head we have made the following division:

Fine arts, properly so called, namely, painting, drawing, sculpture, music.

Industrial and decorative art.

Literature.

In this last division are comprehended works produced by women relating especially to art criticism, the drama, romance, history, etc.

For an exhibit of each of these sections the committee desired that all contributions should be so arranged as to facilitate public inspection, in an attractive and condensed form. To this end all works produced by, or relating to, women have been divided into two classes, both well defined.

First—General statistics embracing the economic and social condition of women in France, together with special accounts of philanthropic works and industrial institutions illustrating these general statistics.

Second—Various articles displaying the labor and talent of the exhibitors.

The main features of the exhibit being thus outlined, the following is the order of details pertaining to each section:

SECTION 1.—EDUCATION. INSTRUCTION.

Here woman is considered as the first instructor, receiving the child from the cradle, rearing, educating, and directing her charge until, in his turn, the object of her care shall be called upon to found a new family. Monographs and general data are supplied relating to children's aid societies, apprenticeships, grades of instruction given to girls, women's education at the time of

EMBROIDERED BROCADE AFTER TAMBOUR WORK OF MARIE ANTOINETTE.
DESIGNED BY LADY HENRY GROSVENOR. ENGLAND.

EMBROIDERED WHITE SATIN CUSHION. PRINCESS LOUISE OF DENMARK.

marriage, diplomas and rewards of merit obtainable, the professions adopted by women, number of elementary schools, both public and private, boarding-schools, professional institutes, colleges, and advanced courses of study.

PAINTING. LOUISE ABBEMA. FRANCE.

A number of specimens of needlework, etc., have been contributed by orphan asylums and working-women's schools.

SECTION 2.—WORKS AND INSTITUTIONS CONNECTED WITH PHILANTHROPY AND SOCIAL ECONOMY.

The committee is convinced that philanthropic labors, which constitute woman's "domain," and in which her heart and intellect

CONDITION DE LA FEMME (TOUTES PROFESSIONS RÉUNIES)

CONDITION OF WOMEN OF FRANCE IN ALL PROFESSIONS.

find so wide a field of profitable endeavor, will prove of the deepest interest.

This second section is devoted to monographs concerning works of private benevolence, such as crèche societies for the rescue and protection of children, orphan asylums, workmen's infirmaries, the occupation of sick-nurses, sisters of charity, deaconesses; to state works, such as women's hospitals, clinics, societies for the aid of wounded soldiers, and health retreats, houses of refuge, of protection, and of correction; societies in aid of penitent liberated convicts, coöperative societies of mutual help, economy, and protection.

Careful study has been bestowed upon the savings of women, the number of bank-depositors, and the sums placed to the credit of women as compared with those of men, the amount of savings in relation to professions, their average amount, and the progress and growth of women's deposits.

Some of the reports furnished by the above-named establishments, at the request of the committee, have been arranged in the form of mural charts, and others have been gathered in an album, entitled an "Album of Women's Work," for the convenient study of the public.

SECTION 3.—WOMEN'S WORK.

The work of women has been classified under the heads of manual, industrial, commercial, administrative, etc.

The committee has carefully ascertained throughout the departments of France the proportion of working-women of all classes, especially those engaged in agriculture and industrial occupations, and the amount of wages gained at different epochs and in different seasons.

The conditions of labor have received particular attention, and with the object of obtaining the desired information a special circular, containing appropriate inquiries, was addressed to those in charge of the principal industrial establishments.

These inquiries regarded the number of women employed, daily hours of labor, wages paid, and societies of social economy intended for the assistance of employes. The replies to these queries are gathered in the album entitled, "Conditions of Labor Among Women."

The tasks intrusted to women in the world of business and the various public and private responsibilities attaching thereto have likewise been classified in the album just spoken of. This includes the services of women in post offices, telegraph and telephone

14

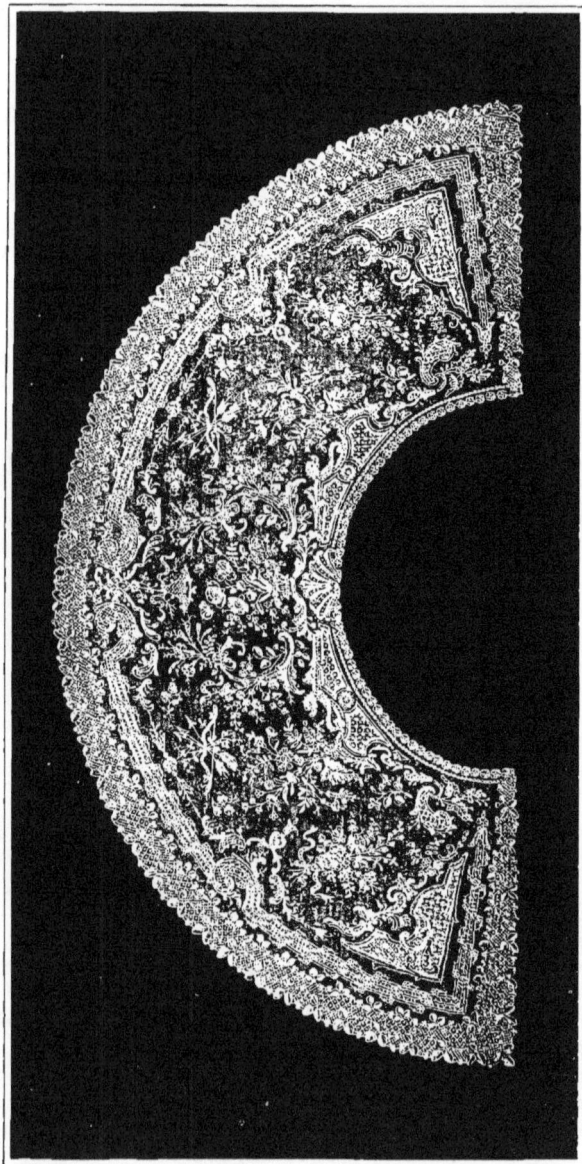

FRENCH ALENÇON POINT LACE FAN. EXHIBITED BY LEFÉBURE. FRANCE.

offices, State manufactories, the Bank of France, the Credit Foncier, the Credit Lyonnais, etc. The great railway companies have supplied the committee with important data bearing upon this subject, which, being incorporated in the reports, can not fail to awaken a lively interest.

With regard to women's work, especially so called, the appeal of the committee has received attention from a considerable number of exhibitors.

Among these works special attention should be called to the lace contributed by the house of M. Lefébure, one article of which, belonging to the Museum of Decorative Art, may justly be considered unique; the embroideries of Mme. Delessert, of the Countess Greffuhle, Mme. Charlotte Georges Ville, Mme. de Clermont-Tonnerre, Mme. Edouard Pailleron, and of the house of Henry. Mention should also be made of the exhibit of N. J. Nayrolles, who displays a portiere which is an exact reproduction of one executed for the president of the French Republic; the curtains of M. Waré; the linen drapery and *robe de chambre* of antique velvet and old Colbert lace of Mme. Franck; infants' wardrobes of Mme. Susse; the embroideries of Mme. Leroudier; the bonnets of Mme. Esther Mayer and M. Auguste Petit; the corsets and petticoats of Mme. Bureau-Bigot; the white embroideries of the house of M. Crouvezier; the gloves of Grenoble; parasols of M. Ahrweiler; the gold embroidery of M. Vaugeois-Binot and M. J. Henry of Lyons; the panels of Mme. Tignet and Mme. Maillot; the large and small screens made by young girls in the house of refuge founded by Mme. Coralie-Cohen at Neuilly-Suresnes; and the flowers of Mme. Boullerot, etc.

The committee, persuaded that the exhibit would be more attractive if the display were set off by an appropriate *entourage*, has designed a charming "*salon régence*," adorned with the following works of art: The tapestry exhibited by M. Braquenié, the "Awakening of Psyche;" a bust of Sophie Arnould, by Mme. Léon Bertaux; a panel by Mme. Leroudier; the Sèvres vase, designed and painted by Mme. Escallier; vases by Mme. Appoil; flowers, Countess Beaulincourt; screen, Countess Greffuhle; basket of orchids, lilacs, and roses from the house of M. Patay; a stand painted by Mme. Gabrielle Neiter; toilettes by Mme. Sarah Meyer and A. Morhauge; the same for young girls, by Mme. Susse; the screen in charcoal-drawing of Mlle. Coesme, and that embroidered by the work-women of the Damon & Colin house; tablecloths, Mme. Franck; decorated *faïence*, Mme. Decamps Sabouret,

EXHIBITS OF LA MAISON HENRY (À LA PENSÉE). FRANCE.

the work of the house of M. Henry; reproductions, chiefly of classic works; and finally the small library of books written by women, comprising women's works, selected by Mme. Jules Siegfried, and giving a more serious tone to the exhibit.

To complete the section a history of French costume, from the period of the Gauls to the present time, has been prepared by the committee, and proves to be full of interest. An exhibit to illustrate the subject has consequently been furnished by the Professional Society l'Aiguille, in the shape of dolls dressed according to authentic records contained in museums, pictures, and documents, and executed with perfect fidelity to historical details.

SECTION 4.—ART.

Feminine art has been considered under two heads—the fine arts, commonly so called, and art applied to decoration and industry.

The number of pictures, drawings, and pieces of sculpture exhibited is not very large, on account of the limited space allotted to each country in the Gallery of Honor of the Woman's Building.

We will here give the names of all the artists exhibiting. These are as follows: Mesdames Madeleine Lemaire, Louise Abbema, Demont Breton, Delphine de Cool, Muraton, la Villette, Marie Bashkirtseff, so truly French in heart and in talent that we have adopted her for one of our own; Mmes. Brouardel Rougier, Buchet, Villebesseyx, Colin Libour, Marquise de Chaponay, Maseline, Türner, Boyer-Breton, Comtesse de Cosse-Brissac, Zillhardt de Châtillon, and others.

In sculpture, we would mention: Mme. Léon Bertaut, two of whose statues, "Psyche Under the Shell of Mystery" and "A Girl Bathing," belong to the collection of the Luxembourg; Mme. Laure Coutan, whose original work, "The Spring," has been purchased by the government; Mme. Anne Manuela, Mme. Clovis Hugues, Mme. Sarah Bernhardt, Mme. Lancelot, and others.

To the above should be added the charcoal sketches of Mme. Mourier, the portrait of Mme. de la Calle, and the engravings of Mlle. Malsis.

In enamels, miniatures, and illuminations we may mention: Mme. Marie de Nugent, Camille Isbert, de Sainté, Anne, Hervé, Garnier, Louvet, Lagoderie, de Cool, Countess du Chaffault, Ernest Moye, Soudan, Montcharmont, etc.

In workmanship shown in the decoration of fans: Mme.

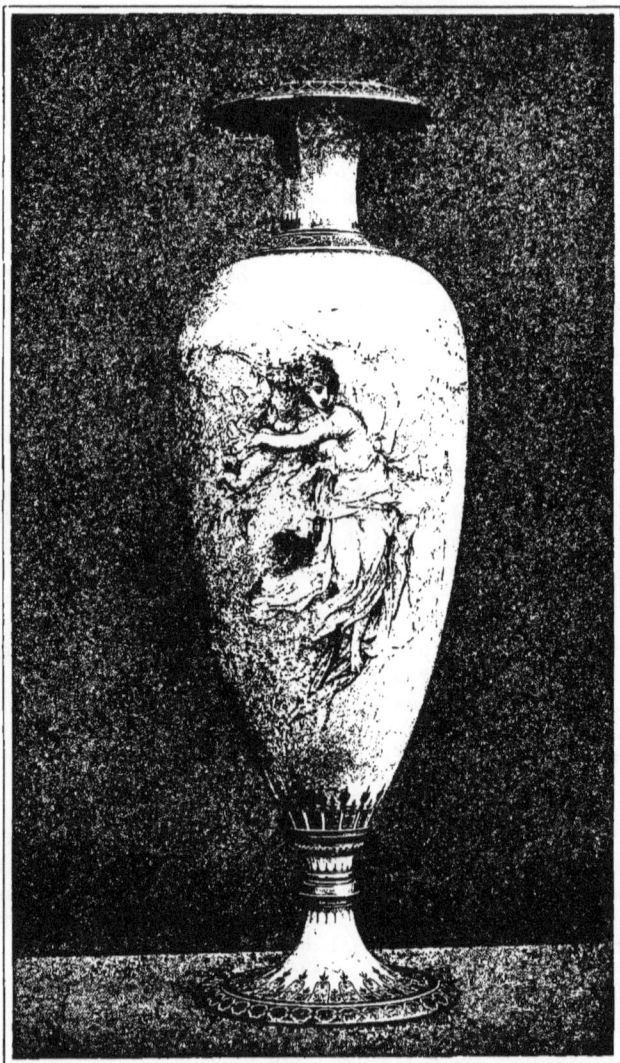

STEPHANUS VASE. YELLOW IVORY BACKGROUND, POLYCHROME PAINTING AND
GOLD DECORATIONS. MME. APOIL. FRANCE.

Abbema, Mme. Chennevieres, Bida and Dumas of the house of Ahrweiler, Baroness de Gartempe, Marquise de Grollier, M. Duvelleroy, etc.

It remains for us to notice the panels intended for the vestibule of one of the grand entrances, the decoration of which was suggested to the French section.

The plan of this was at first received with enthusiasm, especially by Mesdames Van Sarys and Louise Abbema. These ladies were afterward obliged to relinquish this project, but they have desired at least to send to Chicago their designs, which will give a sufficient idea of what the intended panels would have been had their execution been possible.

A list of artists who have exhibited in the Paris Salon appears in one of the charts of the general statistics.

Music is represented by a number of compositions of Vicountess de Grandval, Cecile Chaminade, Augusta Holmes, Marchesi, marchioness of Castrone Rajota, Marie Jaëll, Henriette Fuchs, Hortense Parent, Anna Fabre, Jumel, etc.

Moreover, the various schools of music, the National Conservatory and its branches, together with various national, provincial, and private schools, have kindly forwarded reports touching their organization and course of instruction included in the second album, "Conditions Affecting Women's Work and Professional Instruction."

LITERATURE.

As stated above, a certain number of literary works written by women has been collected by the committee. These works, about eight hundred in all, form the contribution of women authors to the library of the Woman's Building.

In the Gallery of Honor, in the retrospective exhibit, may be seen the antique lace of Mme. Franck, embroidery of the sixteenth century of Mme. John Saulnier, that also of Mmes. Poirier and Rémon, the ivory statuette of Venus lent by Mme. Charles Read, and the valuable collection of forty antique fans of M. Buissot.

In conclusion the committee had wished to add to its exhibit a number of portraits of celebrated women. These, however, for the most part, belonged to public galleries or were the property of private individuals. In either case they were unavailable, in view of so long a transportation; and for this reason the committee has been obliged to content itself with sending photographs, having given preference to personages illustrious in art and letters. The statue of Joan of Arc is the fairest of these reproductions.

SCREEN. EMBROIDERED BY COUNTESS GREFFUHLE, NÉE DE LA ROCHEFOUCAULD. FRANCE.

The committee has also been fortunate enough to obtain permission from Madame Carnot to include her portrait in the exhibit.

And now we may ask whether we have reason to be satisfied with our exhibit, which represents more than eight hundred

OIL PAINTING—"ON THE CLIFF." LOUISE ABBEMA. FRANCE.

exhibitors. The answer is not for us to give, but shall be left to the great number of visitors who will examine it in detail. We may, at least, do ourselves the justice to say that we have spared no pains to render our exhibit worthy of France and of the country which to-day grants us its hospitality, and in which the cause of woman gains daily in recognized importance.

MADAME PEGARD.

NOVI VASE—APPLIED ORNAMENTS, FLOWERS AND BIRDS AND POLYCHROME ENAMEL.
E. RICHARD. FRANCE.

COTTAGE INDUSTRIES IN SCOTLAND AND IRELAND.

THE exhibits of women's work from Scotland and Ireland have been collected respectively by the committees of the Scottish and Irish Home Industries associations, societies which have both been formed within the past two years with the object of promoting and developing home industries among the

CORPORAL VEIL, FLAT NEEDLE-POINT LACE.
PRESENTATION CONVENT INDUSTRY, YOUGHAL, COUNTY CORK. IRELAND.

people, especially in outlying country districts, where the crofters and peasants find so much difficulty in earning their livelihood.

The homespuns made in the highlands and islands of Scotland have long enjoyed a well-deserved reputation, and specimens of these, along with the well-known hand-knitted stockings and gloves, are here on exhibition. A native of Harris has also brought over

SILK EMBROIDERED VESTMENT, MADE FOR HIS GRACE THE ARCHBISHOP
OF IRELAND. ROYAL SCHOOL OF ART EMBROIDERY DUBLIN.

her spinning-wheel, and shows how the soft pure wool from the highland sheep is prepared for the weaver. The far-famed fine Shetland knitted shawls are also represented, not only by specimens from which orders can be taken, but they can be seen in the course of production by a Shetland lassie who will explain the process to onlookers.

But Scotland sends not only specimens of these homely arts (which, however, it must be remembered, are the most permanent as supplying the needs of the many), but exhibits also dainty embroideries from the needles of her daughters in times past and present, for of late years several centers for embroidery-making have sprung up under the encouragement of wise and beneficent ladies.

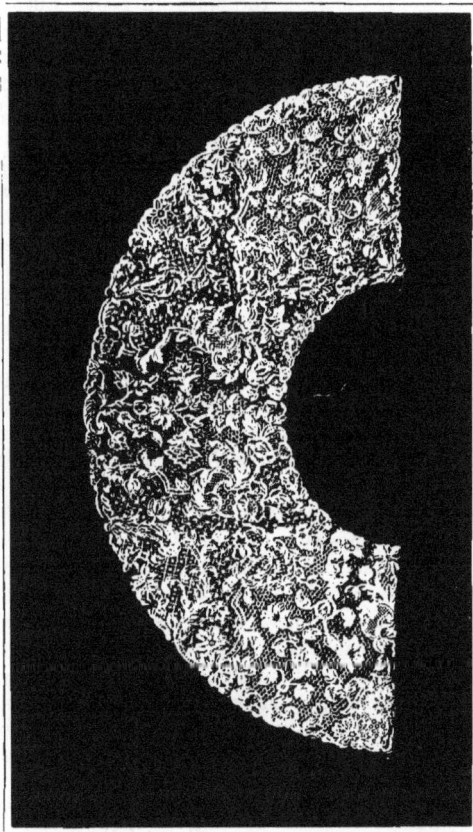

FLAT NEEDLE-POINT LACE FAN COVER. PRESENTATION CONVENT, YOUGHAL, COUNTY CORK, IRELAND.

The Irish case of women's work will be regarded with special interest as showing the perfection to which even such fine work as is needed for ecclesiastical vestments and lace-making can be brought under wise supervision and training.

A great deal of the interest in America, as at home, seems to center round the lace-workers, and truly the history of the origin

of Irish lace-making, as well as its results, is well worthy of the
attention of those interested in the revival of home industries.
Most of the lace-making centers were started during the terrible
famine times of 1847 by charitable ladies intent on finding some
opening for work for the starving poor. Such was the origin of
what became the wide-spread crochet industry in the South of Ireland, and round about Clones in the North, arising from the initiative of the good Ursuline Sisters at Blackrock in the one case, and
in the other of Mrs. Hand, the rector's wife, at Clones. Mrs. Mary
Ann Smith of the Presentation Convent at Youghal found an old
piece of lace and mastered its art herself, and then set to work to
teach it to the poor girls around, who were striving to earn a sub-
sistence on a sort of muslin embroidery long out of date, and at
which a moderately good worker could earn a penny per ten hours.
From this effort has sprung the far-famed beautiful Irish point lace.

Many other instances might be quoted of lace industries arising
out of famine times, but there are two laces which have different
histories, the Carrickmacross and the Limerick. In the year 1820
Mrs. Grey Porter, the wife of the rector of Dunnamoyne, taught
her servant to make lace from a specimen she had brought from
Italy. The circumstance suggested the idea of teaching lace-making to the poor, to a Miss Reid of Radance, near Carrickmacross.
Classes were started, and you can now find scores of cottage-workers
in that district depending mainly on this industry for their living.
It is scarcely possible to conceive how these beautiful laces come
so clean and dainty for bridal array from such poor homes.

The Limerick lace is the one Irish lace which owes its birth to
a spirit of commercial venture. Mr. Charles Walker brought over
twenty-four teachers to Limerick, about 1829, to teach lace-making,
and it became a flourishing business, employing some fifteen
hundred hands. A short time ago I saw one of the original
workers at the lace, an old lady of over eighty, who is proud to tell
of how she is the one survivor of the four women who made Her
Majesty's wedding-veil. Limerick lace is the least expensive of
Irish laces, and when worked out well in a good design is very
pretty, light, and effective. But it fell off in quality of late years,
until Mrs. R. Vere O'Brien set to work to revive it by means of
able supervision and good designs. We greatly hope that this lace
will again come into popular favor, and that our friends in America
will find it suitable for the Easter offerings they give their clergy,
as well as in the embroidered vestments, of which we make so
brave a show at Chicago.

THE GENIUS OF NAVIGATION. —ONE OF THE GROUPS OF STATUARY FLANKING THE
MAIN ARCH OF THE PERISTYLE. BELA L. PRATT OF NEW YORK.

VIEW AT THE NORTH END OF THE LAGOON.

I have quoted these instances of the rise of the lace manufactures, not so much because we wish to lay stress on the lace, but because they afford proof of what great benefits may accrue to a

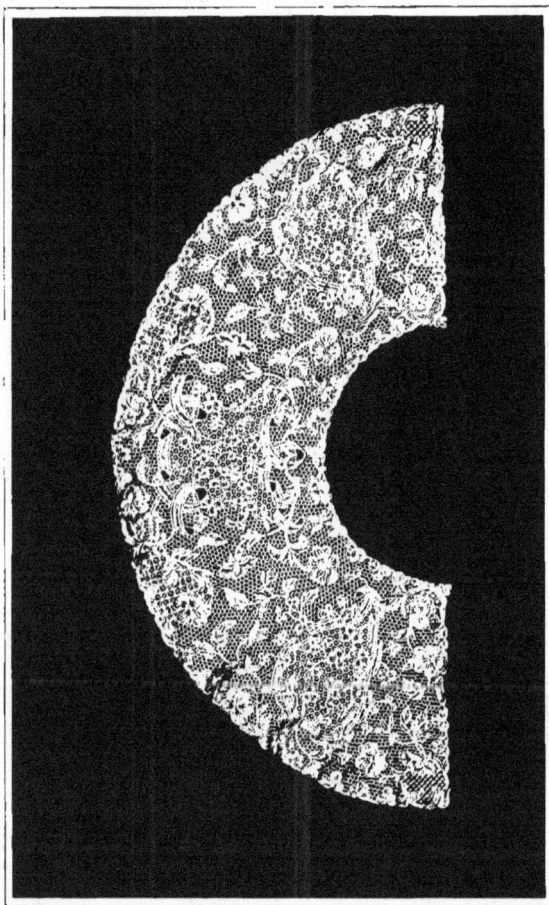

FLAT NEEDLE-POINT LACE FAN COVER. PRESENTATION CONVENT, YOUGHAL, COUNTY CORK, IRELAND.

large number of workers from the humble beginning of one person who desires to help those around in the best way possible, namely, by teaching them to help themselves. The same lesson might be drawn from the experience of a brave and devoted lady, Miss

15

SILK AND GOLD EMBROIDERED VESTMENT, MADE FOR HIS EMINENCE
CARDINAL GIBBONS.
CONVENT OF POOR CLARE'S INDUSTRY, KENMORE, COUNTY KERRY. IRELAND.

Sophy Sturge, who settled down at Letterfrack, in the wild west of Culare, single-handed and amidst many difficulties, to start a basket industry. She began with one pupil, but now has a most flourishing and attractive little industry. Or, take the results which have come to the village of Marlfield, near Clonmel, through the wise and devoted efforts of Mrs. Bagwell, who has the girls in the neighborhood taught every kind of plain needlework, and also embroidery, for which she obtains orders. She makes a condition of her employment of the workers that they should put a certain portion of their earnings in the savings-bank so that they may have a nice little sum put by for their start in life. A very brief visit to the homes of Marlfield, and to other districts where like training has been given, would suffice to prove what has been wrought by such efforts.

These few scattered notes concerning the home industries of Scotland and Ireland will give an idea of the condition of things with which we are striving to deal, and the class of workers whose goods we are bringing before the public. In the meantime we are obliged to provide some outlet into the market for work for which we have not yet found regular trade connections; and this is why we have depots in London (at 20 Motcomb Street, S. W.) and in Dublin (at 14 Suffolk Street), for our Irish work, and at 14 Lower Grosvenor Place, London, for our Scotch work, and why we have sales from time to time. By these means we are making the public acquainted with the excellence of our wares, and we are proud to think that customers who come to us from a charitable desire to help the Scottish and Irish poor, come back to us because they find our work of so good a quality and so moderate in price. A very considerable sum yearly is by these means sent to the homes of the workers, as much as $25,000 having been forwarded last year to the Irish peasants alone. It is difficult to realize, but delightful to contemplate, what comfort and relief this has meant to many, many a home, and we fondly hope that we shall not appeal in vain to our American sisters to take an interest in this undertaking, and to do what in them lies to gain support for it and to help us carry it on and develop it.

ISHBEL ABERDEEN.

EMBROIDERED PORTIERE. J. M. DIXON. ENGLAND.

PHILANTHROPIC WORK OF BRITISH WOMEN.

I VENTURE to hope that the report and exhibit illustrating the philanthropic work of British women, which I have had the honor of presenting to the World's Columbian Exposition, will prove of special interest to those for whom they were prepared. Though it has not been possible to collect materials for a complete and exhaustive record of what British women are doing for the welfare of their fellow beings, I have been enabled by the kind coöperation of a very large number of correspondents and writers to bring together sufficient information to form a report upon the philanthropic work promoted or originated by British women, which I trust will not only be found instructive and useful, but of permanent value.

The report comprises three distinct features. Of these the first is a volume of Congress papers entitled "Woman's Mission," printed and published for general circulation by Messrs. Sampson Low, Marston & Co. of London, and Messrs. Charles Scribner's Sons of New York. The second is a series of type-written reports, bound up in six folio volumes, which are lodged for reference and perusal in the space allotted to me in the Woman's Building. These type-written volumes may be said to form the basis of the printed volume, "Woman's Mission," as they contain the whole body of information in the form in which it was received from authoritative sources. This information is embodied in the printed volume of Congress papers, which have been written by the following ladies, whose ability and experience have enabled them not only to deal with the many important questions under notice, but to supplement the material contained in the type-written reports by additional information derived from personal knowledge:

H. R. H. Princess Christian of Schleswig-Holstein, Mrs. Alexander, Miss Anne Beale, Miss Violet Brooke-Hunt, Baroness Burdett-Coutts, Miss Fanny L. Calder, Mrs. Boyd Carpenter, Countess Compton, Mrs. Charles Garnett, Mrs. Gilbert (Rosa Mulholland), Mrs. Cashel Hoey, Miss Louisa M. Hubbard, Miss Emily Janes, Hon. Mrs. Muir Mackenzie, Lady Victoria Lambton, Miss E. S.

Lidgett, Mrs. Malleson, Miss Marsh, Mrs. Molesworth, Miss Florence Nightingale, Miss Petrie, B. A., Mrs. G. A. Sala, the authoress of "The Schonberg–Cotta Family;" Miss E. Sellers, Hon. Maude

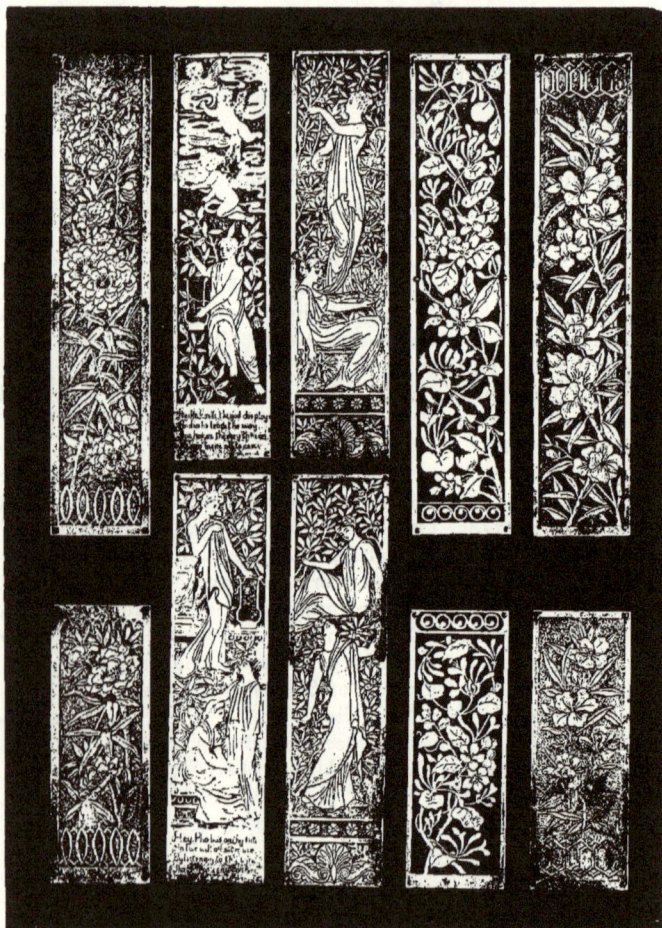

FIVE PAIRS OF FINGER PLATES. VIOLET M. PARKER. ENGLAND.

Stanley, Miss Mary Steer, Miss Hesba Stretton, Mrs. Sumner, Miss Louisa Twining, Miss Agnes E. Weston, Hon. Mrs. Stuart Wortley. The third feature of my exhibit is the collection shown in the

Woman's Building of specimens of work done in various philanthropic institutions, together with a number of models, sketches, photographs, maps, and some seventy printed volumes of reports, etc.   All the examples of work exhibited—though in some instances of comparatively small value—possess a history.   Taken in association with the written report presented to the exhibition, they tell many a story of how single individuals setting to work with heart and mind, and pursuing the effort with courage and tact, can conquer the obstacles presented by an isolated and resourceless district, by an ignorant and untrained population, by an apathy and idleness arising mainly from the want of hopeful inspiration and skilled guidance.   They are so many proofs, these little pieces of handiwork, of the industry and cleverness which lie buried in the poorest classes, and the effective materialization of which is one of the best and most reproductive objects to which philanthropic effort can be applied—for the work required in the production does not end with the object produced, and the reward is not to be measured by the little wage given in return, in itself often an appreciable help to the scanty resources of a struggling family.   It carries on into the future; it implies that the hand which hitherto was unskilled has been trained to execute, and the eye to select and discriminate.   The mind as well as the body has learned the habit of work, and the whole *morale* of the individual is braced and trained.

Upon the methods adopted for collecting the information contained in the printed and type-written volumes, it is not necessary for me to dwell here.   Those who are interested in the subject will find the information given in detail in my preface to " Woman's Mission," where I have also explained why the Columbian Exposition will, in my opinion, give to 1893 a significant and unique place in the history of the material and social progress of the world. Hitherto international exhibitions have been chiefly concerned with the material progress of civilization.   At Chicago the moral and social progress of the world receives a prominent and peculiar consideration.   Moreover, under this second head, the department of woman's work takes its place for the first time, and both on that account and by reason of the special regard given to philanthropy much of the deeper and more lasting interest excited by this great Exhibition will, I think, gather round the section for which this report has been prepared.   It is fitting that the close of the nineteenth century should focus and illustrate in a definite form the share which women have taken in its development, of which, in

TERRA COTTA STATUETTE—"BOY AND DOG." R. A. FRASER TYTLER. ENGLAND.

my humble judgment, the truest and noblest, because the most natural, part is to be found in philanthropic work.

In conclusion, I venture to hope that the information upon the philanthropic work of British women which I have been able to present to the Chicago Exposition will not be unwelcome in the country for which it was collected. My personal feeling and knowledge, to quote once more from my preface to "Woman's Mission," have led me to believe that the past and present work of English women would have for the American people an attraction exceeding any felt by other nations, however interested these may be in a common charity. In an unusual degree the blood of many races runs in our veins; but we are bound together in the one

CARVED WOOD PANEL FROM RECORD ROOM. K. E. P. MOSHER. UNITED STATES.

historic record of the English-speaking peoples. One language unites us; one Bible, one literature. The poetry and prose of past centuries, and the first achievements of Englishmen in the dim twilight of scientific discovery, are a common heritage of both nations. In the past fifty years the genius of both, sometimes divided, sometimes intermingled, has kept the light burning. To the sacred lamp of literature American authors have added a peculiar radiance of their own, and the field of discovery and invention has been illuminated by the splendid achievements of American research. And as in these two great branches of progress we are at once co-inheritors and fellow-workers, so the philanthropic work of English women, commingled by practice and example with the work of American women, must, I feel, have an absorbing interest for those who, like ourselves, have drawn their national being from the Anglo-Saxon race.

THE BARONESS BURDETT-COUTTS.

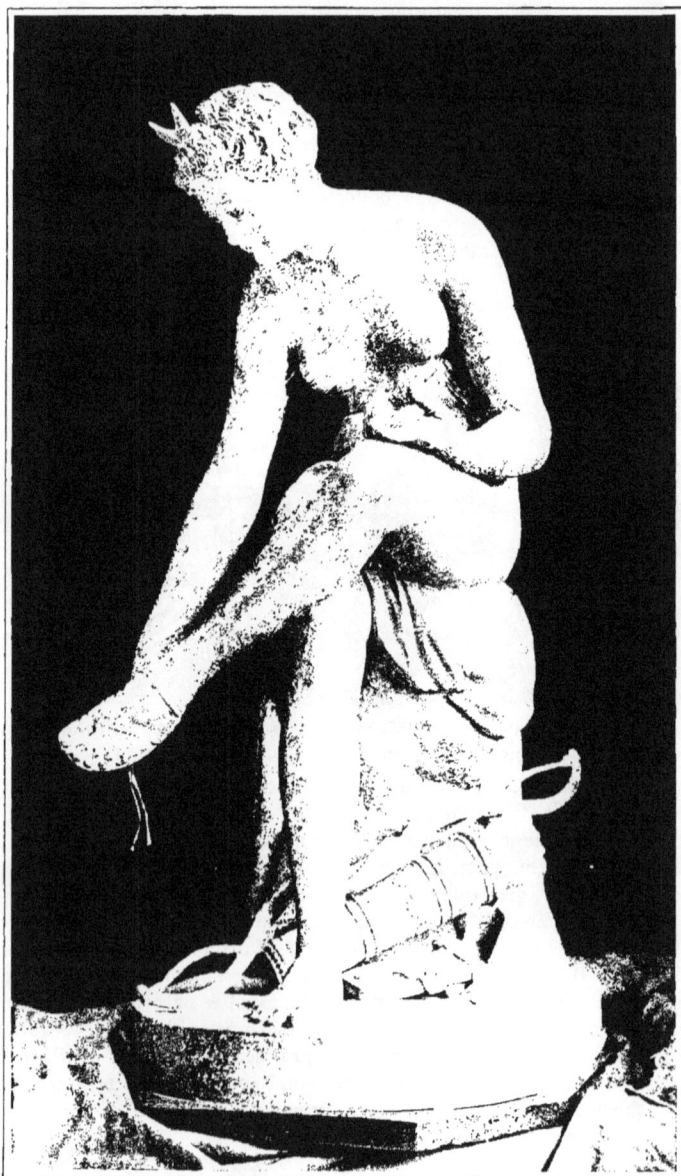

DIANA—STATUE. Miss Grant. England.

GREAT BRITAIN — ART.

GREAT Britain is justly proud of her women artists, some of whom are represented in the Woman's Building, but to judge of all that they are exhibiting at Chicago, the visitor must look in at the Art Palace and see some of the strong pictures exhibited there. It is nothing new to find English women in the front ranks of British art. They have always held a distinguished position, and in any book which pretends to give the history of women's achievements in art a very large proportion of the painters will be found to have been English, either by birth or by adoption. It is interesting to remember that a woman painter was one of the original members of the Royal Academy, whose charter was signed by King George III., at the instance of the American painter Benjamin West, who, after the death of Sir Joshua (first president of the Academy), held the position of president during the remainder of his life. In the art exhibitions of London, women to-day hold a prominent position. Mrs. Alma Tadema is a painter with a great deal of originality and of power. Her husband has been heard to say that his highest ambition is to have it written on his tombstone, " Here lies the husband of Mrs. Alma Tadema." Mrs. Stillman is one of our popular painters. Her pictures possess a certain ideal quality which is not always to be found combined with the admirable technique which we find in her work. Miss Lena Stillman, one of our younger artists, is full of promise. There is a certain gravity and dignity about her compositions which win for them immediate recognition. Kate Greenaway's name is a household word. Her delightful illustrations are known in every home where children and good taste are to be found. She has done more, perhaps, to bring about an improvement in the dress of our little men and little maids than any other individual. One meets whole groups of Kate Greenaway children in Hyde Park on a Sunday morning. Mrs. George Watts has achieved a reputation by her admirable portraits.

In the use of water-colors, women share the high position that our English artists hold in that exquisite branch of art, for there

BOOK COVER; PULPIT HANGING; PRAYER BOOK COVER OF CHARLES I. BELONGING TO H. M. THE QUEEN. ENGLAND,

can be no denying that in aquarelles no school has ever approached the English. The opportunities for studying art in our country are very great, for women as well as for men. The careless observer, judging only from the large annual exhibitions, in which it may be held that the standard is not kept sufficiently high, may be inclined to underrate contemporary British art, but the careful student will find that London is in fact, as well as in name, one of the great art centers of the world. While George Watts, Walter Crane, and Burne-Jones live, we can claim that in the field of portraiture, illustration, and ideal work three of the greatest contemporary artists are English born and bred. The Montalba sisters, Mrs. Adrian Stokes, Blanche Jenkins, Henrietta Rae, Miss Osborne, and Miss Stewart Wood are well represented at Chicago. Mrs. Swynnerton's " Mater Triumphalis " at the Art Palace wins almost as much commendation as Lady Butler's famous picture, " The Roll Call." When this was exhibited for the first time at the Royal Academy, a policeman was in attendance to keep the crowd in order that always gathered about it. The picture was bought by Her Majesty Queen Victoria, who has kindly consented to send it to Chicago.

Mrs. Adrian Stokes exhibits two of her important pictures, an " Annunciation," very original in composition, and a pathetic little scene which she calls " Go, thou must play alone, my boy." A little lad sits weeping bitterly beside his playmate, who lies at rest white and still as the flowers on her breast. The treatment of this familiar subject is very tender, the dead child is exquisitely painted, and the grief of the little brother is quiet, reserved, and infinitely human. The women sculptors who exhibit are Miss B. A. M. Brown, Miss Henrietta Montalba, Miss Ada M. Chignell, and Miss E. M. Moore. Among the etchings and engravings excellent examples of the work of Mrs. Dale, Miss Ethel Martyn, and Miss Elizabeth Piper may be found. When the exceedingly high standard of the work which Great Britain has sent to Chicago is taken into account, it is a significant and encouraging fact that forty-five women are represented among the British artists exhibiting in the Art Palace.

The east vestibule of the Woman's Building is decorated by two large mural paintings. The one by Mrs. Swynnerton represents three different phases of nursing, the care of the young, the sick, and the aged. The decoration is in the form of a triptych. The central panel represents the Crimean Hospital at Scutari, with the sick and wounded soldiers lying on

MARQUETRY SCREEN. LENT BY THE WORKING LADIES' GUILD. ENGLAND.

their pallet beds, their faces turned toward the single gracious figure of Florence Nightingale standing in their midst, a figure full of dignity and of pathos. It was in this hospital that the dying boy kissed the shadow of Florence Nightingale as it fell upon the wall by his bed. In one of the smaller panels we have a handsome, robust young mother with a lusty child upon her knee, while the remaining one shows us the figure of an aged woman; beside her sits her young granddaughter. One feels here that the situation is reversed; the young girl is repaying something of the care and love which in her infancy were lavished upon her. There is a wealth of sentiment and tenderness in this three-fold presentation of woman's great duty and prerogative, the care of the weak and helpless. Facing Mrs. Swynnerton's decoration are three corresponding panels by Mrs. Anna Lee Merritt, who, though by birth an American, has for so long lived and worked in England that we may fairly claim her for one of our painters. The central panel is a spirited scene, representing woman the mistress of the needle. A group of seated figures about an embroidery frame is particularly worthy of notice. In the right-hand panel a group of fair girl graduates receive their diplomas from the hand of a college dignitary. It is interesting to learn that the process used by Mrs. Merritt in this decoration is a novel one which has only lately been known in England. The whole work was executed between the 1st of February and the 8th of April, which gives us an idea of the artist's industry. In justice to Mrs. Swynnerton and Mrs. Merritt, it should be said that their work is seen at something of a disadvantage owing to the narrowness of the vestibule in which it is placed. It would be seen at a much better advantage at a far greater distance than is here possible. Miss Clara Montalba exhibits a charming little picture of the palace in Venice where Robert Browning lived, and from whence his body was carried in that wonderful funeral pageant when the English poet, lying in his flower-crowned barge, was carried down the Lido, followed by all the dignitaries and notables of Venice. Hilda Montalba's "Market Woman of Dordrecht" is clever and well drawn, and deserves the commendation which it received when it was exhibited last year in the Royal Academy. Miss Alice Grant's " Portrait of a Baby " shows us a jolly little wight, full of fun and good humor. Mrs. Perugini's " Portrait of a Child " is a characteristic piece of work. The " Sussex Cottage " by Mrs. Allingham and the charming landscape by Miss Stewart Wood have been widely admired. Henrietta Rae's large picture of " Eurydice Sinking

Back into Hades " is a very powerful composition. The artist has chosen the moment when the beloved shade vanishes from the eyes of the agonized Orpheus and sinks sadly and mutely back to the nether world from which his insistent adjurations have summoned her.

In sculpture women are achieving as great a success in England as they are in France and in the United States. One of the most beautiful pieces of sculpture exhibited last year in London was the

CUSHION. DESIGNED BY H. R. H. THE PRINCESS LOUISE. ENGLAND.

bas-relief of " Silene," shown at the Royal Academy by one of our leading women sculptors. Her Royal Highness the Princess Louise has won distinction both in painting and in sculpture. Her portrait of Paderewski and the bust of her royal mother, exhibited last year, merited the high praise they received.

In needlework and embroidery our women have never been surpassed, and it is a cause of great satisfaction to us to learn that the Kensington school, which has done so much to improve the art of the needle in Great Britain, has extended its potent influence throughout the United States, and that the leading schools of needlework in this country acknowledge that they owe their very existence to the Kensington school.

In music we are not behind. Virginia Gabriel's songs have had a wide and well-deserved popularity, shared by the compositions of Elizabeth Philp. Among our younger composers, two of the most eminent, Rosalind Ellicott and Ethel Smythe, have contributed manuscript copies of some of their best-known works.

In commerce woman is taking every day a more prominent place. In the old days, the only refuge for a reduced gentlewoman was the profession of a governess or companion, but to-day we find many women of good family who find in trade an excellent and dignified means of self-support. Several ladies of rank, as is very well known, have opened millinery and dressmaking establishments.

In philanthropic work Englishwomen have long been prominent, while in literature they have maintained the high position won for them by Maria Edgeworth, George Eliot, Elizabeth Barrett Browning, and the Brönte sisters. Among our most popular novelists to-day are Miss Braddon, Ouida, Rhoda Broughton, Mrs. Lynn Linton, Mrs. Alexander, Mrs. Humphrey Ward, and the late Miss Edwards, whose fame as an archæologist has almost eclipsed her work in literature. Frances Power Cobb is a name worthy to close this very imperfect survey of the women who to-day are among the leading spirits in the fields of intellectual labor. The work of women may be likened to the labor of the coral insects who for centuries toil unseen and unnoticed beneath the ocean of oblivion. At last a day comes when the winds and the waves bring their tribute of soil, the passing birds drop the seeds of tree and flower, and of a sudden a fair island rises from the sea, with fruit and foliage and pleasant streams. The navigator discovers the new land and writes it down on his chart, and the patient toil of the untold myriads of insects is at last rewarded.

E. CRAWFORD.

Mrs. Crawford, the writer of this paper, exhibits one of the most striking pictures in the Hall of Honor, a large water-color painting of a Roman scene; a nun passing up a marble stairway, and looking back at a cheerful young peasant woman leading a rosy child and carrying a funeral wreath. The colors used in this work are of a new manufacture, and attention is called to the reds, which have proved very satisfactory.—ED.

16

"THE END OF THE HOP HARVEST." Miss Stuart Wood, England.

BRITISH NURSES' EXHIBIT.

THERE is no more important and, I believe, no more interesting exhibit in the Woman's Building than that made by the British Royal Commission on professional nursing. The pleasant room leading from the gallery in which the exhibit is installed is graced by a portrait of Her Majesty the Queen, which bears her signature. A portrait of H. R. H. Princess Christian of Schleswig-Holstein, and one of the Princess Helena, find a place near by. The Queen is a patron of the Jubilee Institute for Nurses, while the Princess Helena is president of the Royal British Nurses' Association. The interest taken by these august personages is a very real one, and is shared by many of our most-distinguished women.

Though we must consider that Sarah Gamp was, perhaps, an exceptionally ignorant type of nurse, it must be admitted that in drawing her character Dickens can not be accused of having made a caricature. How different a class of woman is now intrusted with the sacred task of nursing the sick, one has but to examine the exhibit to realize. The neat, suitable uniforms of the British nurses, the appliances they use, the various inventions they have made for the sick-room, can not fail to prove to the most careless observer that the profession to which these things appertain is both honorable and scientific. Attention is called to the medical and surgical dressings, the bandages and belts arranged by Mrs. Walter Lakin, the hygienic clothing for nurses made by Miss Franks, the splints padded by nurses, the model of a hygienic room for the instruction of nurses designed by Mrs. Lionel Pridgin Teale, the nurse's toilet basket and the glass appliances for sterilized surgical dressings designed by Mrs. Bedford-Fenwick. The surgical models, designed and made by sister Marion Turnball of the London Homeopathic Hospital deserve notice, as do Miss Simpson's basket, used by the "Princess Christian's Nurses," and the bag used by the "Queen's Nurses."

These exhibits are not only interesting in themselves, but are instructive evidences of the immense strides made in nursing

CURIO TABLE AND CHEST IN STAINED MARQUETRY. EXHIBITED BY THE WORKING LADIES' GUILD. ENGLAND.

during this century. Twenty years ago, nursing as a profession for woman was practically unrecognized. Very few, except those who were unable to obtain any other means of livelihood, could be induced to undertake it. So pressing had the need become that a suggestion was made by some eminent authorities to meet it by training the numerous able-bodied women in work-houses as nurses for the sick. This plan, though never carried into effect, was useful in opening up the way for other and more practical schemes, and to-day we see women of all classes anxious to enroll themselves in the band of trained workers. Many of course are possessed of very indifferent qualifications. At present there is no uniformity of training in Great Britain, more especially with regard to the length of time which must elapse before a nurse can be certified as fully trained. There is nothing to hinder any woman from putting on a uniform after a few months' sojourn in a hospital or infirmary, and calling herself a trained nurse. To

EMBROIDERED VELLUM FRAME.
BOSTON SOCIETY OF DECORATIVE ART.

protect the public against untrustworthy persons of this type, an association was formed about five years ago, with Her Royal Highness Princess Christian at its head, called the Royal British Nurses' Association, which undertakes to register all nurses who have undergone *three* years' instruction in the practice and theory of nursing in a recognized institution. Thus, at a moment's glance, any one can satisfy themselves as to the qualifications of the nurse they wish to employ. The registration board not only inquires into the educational process through which a nurse has passed, but is the result of a most careful and painstaking scrutiny into her character and antecedents as well. There is no doubt that under the ægis of a royal charter it will exercise a powerful influence of an educational nature on professional and public opinion, and thus prepare the way for those further advances in the organization and training of nurses which it is the main object of the association to promote.

MRS. BEDFORD-FENWICK.

OIL PAINTING—"CHRIST AND THE SINNER." COUNTESS KALKREUTH, GERMANY.

GERMANY.

IN anticipation of the World's Columbian Exposition in Chicago, in 1893—the first international exhibition which has presented a comprehensive review of all that woman has done in the domains of art, science, industry, education, charity, and philanthropy—the Imperial Commissioner called together, in the spring of 1892, a number of leading German women. From these a central committee was formed, under the patronage of Her Imperial Highness the Princess Frederick Charles. Headquarters were established in Berlin, and a large number of sub-committees were appointed in different parts of the German Empire. The officers of this committee are: Mrs. Schepeler-Lette, president; Miss Lange, vice-president; Mrs. Kaselowsky, secretary; Mrs. Dr. Tiburtius, assistant secretary; and Mrs. Schrader, treasurer. The following ladies accepted the position of honorary president: Countess von Pueckler, the wife of State Minister Delbrueck, and the wife of State Minister von Schelling. The central committee consists of the presidents of all the German sub-committees. Among its members are: Miss von Cotta, Mrs. Jessen, Mrs. Noeldechen, Miss von Hobe, Miss Fuhrmann, Miss von Keudell, Mrs. Heyl, Mrs. Morgenstern, and Mrs. Vely, from Berlin; Mrs. Simson and Mrs. Dr. Asch of Breslau, Mrs. Weber of Tuebingen, and Mrs. Bonhoefer of Stuttgart.

Separate committees, the members of which are too numerous to mention, have labored with untiring energy. Thanks to their efforts Germany has been able to make an exceptionally complete exhibit in the Woman's Building. There are there represented products and models relating to commerce, manufactures, cooking schools, house-keeping schools (schools in domestic economy), Froebel's kindergartens and seminaries, schools for little children, high schools and scientific institutes, home missions, hospital service, hygiene, eating-houses for the poor, printing, photography, art, horticulture, etc.

A valuable addition, which should notably facilitate the study of this contribution to the Exposition, consists of the statistical

PORTRAIT. VILMA PARLAGHY. GERMANY.

reports and the numerous accounts, programmes, and prospectuses which illustrate woman's work in commerce, manufacture, art, printing, photography, and horticulture, as well as in many branches of philanthropy and education. Much also may be learned of the kindergarten system, schools of domestic economy, the hospitals and charitable institutions.

Considering the amount of space allotted to them the women painters make a very good showing. The photographs of eminent dramatic artists and singers form an interesting feature of the exhibit. Authors are represented by some four hundred volumes, collected by Mrs. C. Vely and Miss Jennie Hirsch. At the close of the Exhibition these books will be given to the Women's Memorial Library.

The statistical tables prepared by Mrs. Dr. Gnauck-Kuehne give a comprehensive account of the social status and occupations of the German working-women, and are especially interesting.

The exhibit of the German women is most satisfactory, not only from its wide range and quantity, but also from its excellent quality. The diligence with which the best has been brought together also deserves high appreciation. The art exhibit is particularly interesting; it includes two works by Her Royal Highness the Princess Frederick Carl, which add an especial charm. We find a wide range of subject and treatment: the Countess Kathrenth is represented by a painting of "Christ and the Sinner," while Mrs. Biber-Boehm exhibits her picture of "Ahasverus."

Among the portraits we have Vilma Parlarghy's well-known and admirable picture of herself in a charming costume of white satin. Near by hangs a portrait of the famous poet and painter Marie von Olfers, by Fraulein Strempel. Dora Flitz's picture, a mother and child, proves the artist to belong to the impressionist school. Fraulein Lübbes' picture, "Lost in Thought," is particularly strong in color.

Among the landscapes M. von Keudell's delicately executed "Bluemli's Alp" deserves attention, and Mrs. Begas Parmentier's study of Venice is a charming composition. Frau Von Preuschen's "Elaine" represents the lily maid of Astolat lying in her flower-strewn barge. We must also commend Clara Lobedan's "Italian Grapes," and the works of Hildegard Lehnert, Frau Kallmorgen, and Fraulein Ley.

Particularly, however, the attention of admirers of flowers is called to Katharine Klein's "Roses," the perfume of which one seems to inhale. In this connection may be mentioned a glass case

EMBROIDERY ON WHITE SATIN. GERMANY.

of fans, the majority of which have been already awarded prizes in Karlsruhe. We will only mention among them the works of the following ladies: Erler, Laudien, Wedekind, Ankermann, and Wittmann, and regret that space does not allow a more detailed description. A large chest of drawers placed in the immediate vicinity of the fans contains many exquisite embroideries of different styles, nearly all of them works of the highest order. Among them is one of white satin, with many-colored embroidery, in the style of the Renaissance, by Miss Barbara Wolf; also a large bed-cover executed with ebony-colored cordonet silk in open embroidery; some artistic hand-work from the atelier of the Lette Club; an ornamental pillow by Mrs. von Wedel, executed in the most exquisite manner, with gold silk and applique on red satin, as well as a rich collection of covers and pillows of various styles, among which the fine work of Mrs. Gerson deserves mention. A wall-hanging about 19⅔ feet square, executed in gobelin embroidery, is unique and beautiful. The design was taken from an old motif of the fifteenth century. This is also by Miss Wolf.

Germany has always been distinguished by the excellence of her schools, and they are worthily represented by the exhibits of the Sophien Institute of Weimar, the public schools of Breslau and Munich, the working-women's school of Reutlingen, the high school of Rheydt, the Women's Educational Club of Breslau, and the Lette Club of Berlin. All these institutions offer numerous illustrations of their achievements in the field of woman's hand-work. The case of the latter illustrates also the great extent of the field covered by its institutes, which include the commercial and photographic schools that provide secure positions in life for a large number of young girls. In this connection a small exhibit of lace from the school at Schmiedeberg may be mentioned, as it illustrates the many processes of lace-making. In this school was manufactured the point lace of the silver wedding-dress of Her Majesty the Empress Friedrich, presented by the ladies of Silesia. This lace may be seen in the exhibit.

The "People's Kitchen" and the "Household Schools" of Mrs. Morgenstern are shown in three small models, while certain statistical tables compiled by the same lady are exceedingly valuable. A child's cooking-stove, with stove furniture, a charming model of the kindergarten in Breslau, the school for little children in Siegersdorf, all demonstrate what has been done in this field.

Among works of charity we find: Pictures of hospitals, exhibited by the Woman's Club of Baden, the patroness of which is the

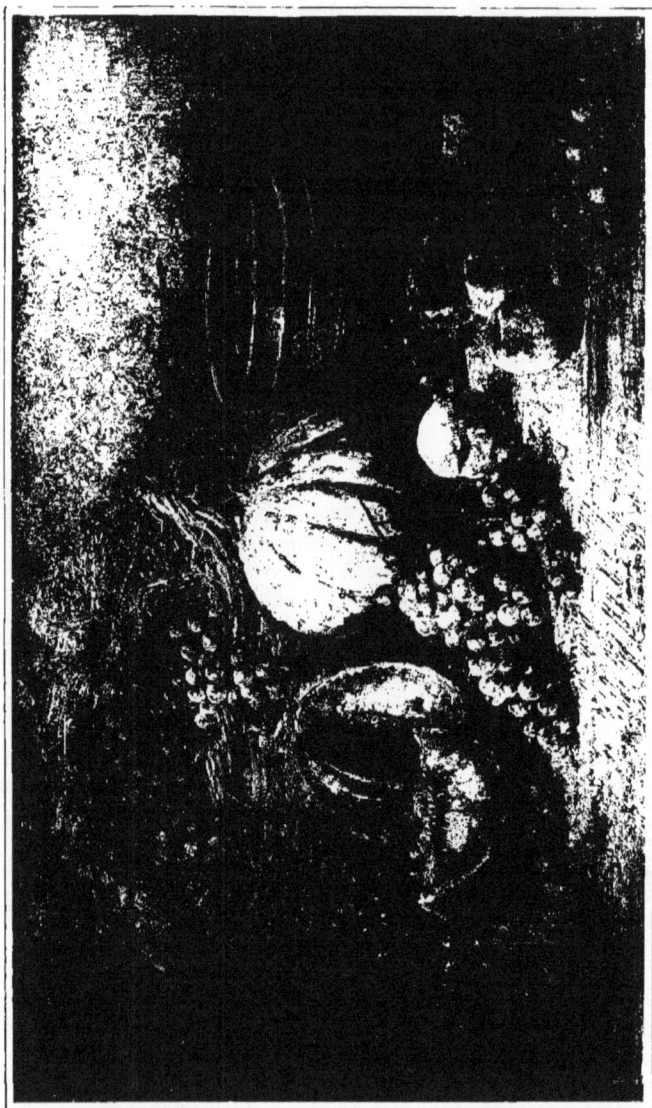

OIL PAINTING—FRUIT. MOLLY CRAMER. GERMANY.

grand duchess; models of the dresses of the female nurses, besides a number of statistical tables from Berlin, and the charitable gifts of the mission club "Edelweiss." To our great regret the exhibit of the "Pestalozzi Froebel Institute" has been placed in the Liberal Arts Building, separated from our main exhibit, the space for which was too limited; it is executed in a most artistic manner,

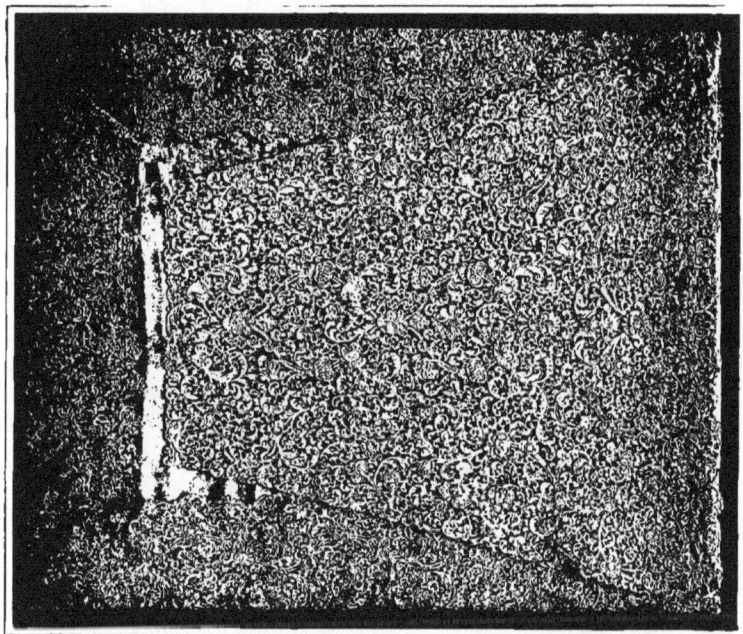

PART OF LACE DRESS. EX-EMPRESS FREDERICK. GERMANY.

and close inspection indicates the devoted fulfillment of the educational mission of the institute.

Last, not least, must be mentioned the books which have been presented to the ladies of America, and are to be found in the library of the Woman's Building. The reputation of women like Fanny Lewald, Louise von François, Emily Erhart, Natalie von Eschstruth, Louise von Droste-Huelshoff, Hermine von Hillern, Tekla von Gumpert, Ottilie Wildermuth, E. Vely, and others, is an assurance that the women authors of Germany deserve the high reputation which they have won.

MADAME KASELOWSKY.

THE GENIUS OF DISCOVERY. — ONE OF THE GROUPS OF STATUARY FLANKING THE
MAIN ARCH OF THE PERISTYLE. BELA L. PRATT OF NEW YORK.

OIL PAINTING—FLOWERS. FRAULEIN LEY. GERMANY.

Engraved by Rand, McNally & Co.   SPRING --STATUE.   CANADA.

SPAIN.

THE display made by the Spanish women in the Woman's Building of the World's Columbian Exposition, although one of the most important in that department, suffers very much on account of the lateness of the action taken in Spain to gather specimens of the work and labor of women.

By an unfortunate circumstance, there had not been a Spanish Minister in Washington for some time until the end of 1892. The American Minister left his post in Madrid also at the same time; and besides this there was in Spain a change in the government.

Her Majesty the Queen did not know the importance of the Exposition and the desire of the Board of Lady Managers until a very few weeks before the opening of the Fair, and it has been very difficult to gather, in such a short time, a comprehensive collection of what woman is doing in Spain.

Immediately her majesty had knowledge of the desires of the American ladies, she surrounded herself with the ladies most accustomed to manage affairs of that sort, because of the part they take in charities, education, and in the literary and intellectual movement, and calling together the ladies of the different provinces, in a very few days they gathered what is to be seen in the pavilion of Spain in the Woman's Building.

The women of Spain have always played a very important part in the social development of the country, and in the growth of the nation. The status of woman in Spain, her position and influence in the family and in the government, does not originate only in the gallantry that is always accorded to Spain by people who think of our country with romantic ideas, but is due to the Christian principle that woman is the equal of man.

The law of the country gives equal rights to rule to women and to men, and Spain boasts of such queens as Isabella the Catholic, Maria de Molina, and the present Queen Regent, who have given her the greatest days of glory, and the best government under very difficult circumstances; and of queens and mothers like the two sisters

17 (257)

SPANISH LACE WITH THE ARMS OF CHARLES V. EXHIBITED BY LADY LAYARD, ITALY.

Blanca and Berenguela, mothers of two great kings and two saints, San Ferdinand of Spain and Saint Louis of France.

The law gives to woman such a prominent place in the family that we have what is called *los gananciales*—that is to say, the gains in marriage; this implies that the augmentation of the fortune of man and wife, during their married life, has to be equally divided, for the law wisely thinks that the wife and mother, by her economy, her making the home pleasant, and her devotion to the education of her children, plays a part as important as the husband in making the fortune of the family.

She has, after the death of her father, the *patria potestad*, and she has by right a portion equal to the one inherited by each of the children.

The short space given to each nation in this book makes it impossible to fully portray the importance of woman in the history of Spain, but it is easy to say, that although her character makes her principally a home-abiding woman, that although she is retiring and avoids publicity, and dislikes all that is noisy and seems to her immodest, she has all the rights of man except the political rights. She has the right to take the highest honors in the government universities, and avails herself of it; she takes an important part in the productive industry of the country, both as merchant and worker; she does creative work in literature and art, directs the education of children in the elementary schools, and is recognized as the most active worker in charities by the state, which has given to a commission of ladies the direction of the hospitals and asylums.

The women of Spain have always shown that they can do everything that men can do. They have fought the enemies of the country heroically, like Maria Pita and Augustina de Aragon, they have stood by their husbands and sons in sieges and battles, being a source of strength, and never a pretext for weakness. As far back as the fifteenth century we find such philosophers as Teresa de Cartagena, and learned women as Beatriz Galindo, the friend and adviser of the great Queen Isabella, who was called "*La Latina*" from her achievements in classic literature.

In the pavilion erected in the Woman's Building by the Spanish Commission, can be read the names of eight women who have been celebrated not only in Spain, but are known by every educated person all over the world: Santa Teresa de Jesus, one of the classic writers of Spanish literature, whose writings on philosophical matters have had a great influence; Oliva Sabuco de Nantes,

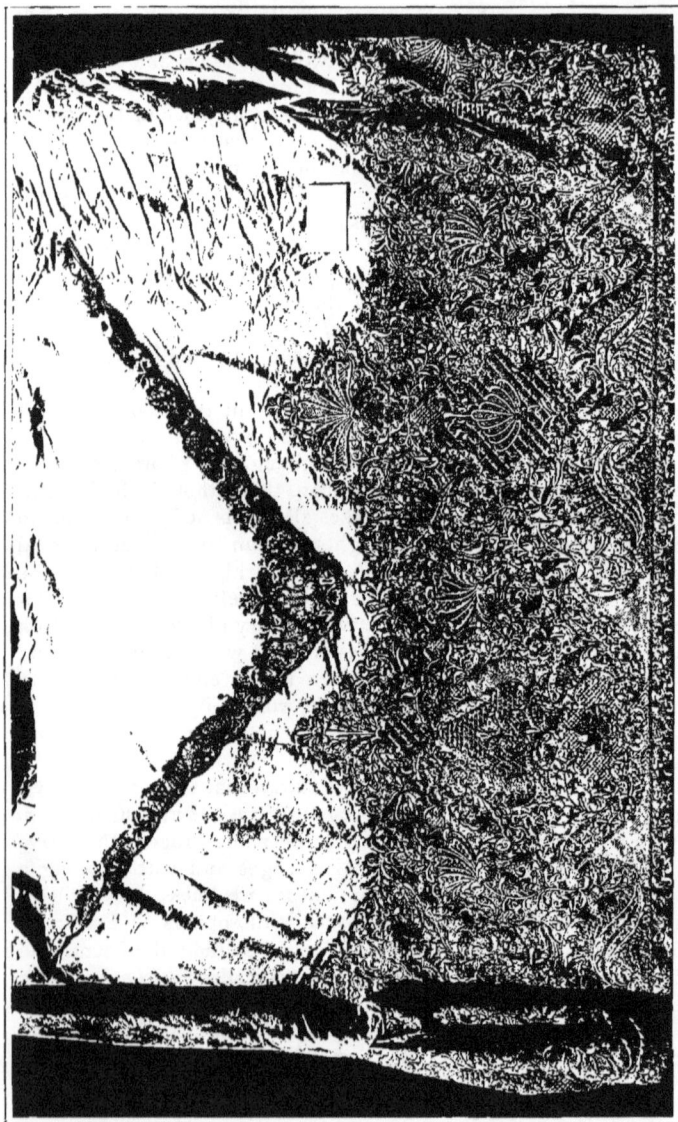

GOLD EMBROIDERY XVI CENTURY. EXHIBITED BY THE COUNTESS DI BRAZZA, ITALY.

whose treaty on the "New Philosophy of Man and Nature" was printed in 1587; Sor. Maria de Agreda, author of the celebrated book "La Mistica Ciudad de Dios," and who carried on correspondence with Philip IV., King of Spain, leaving letters that are a treasure of wisdom in political and state matters. Many names have had to be omitted which in justice should have been given with the others—if space had allowed—such as the names of the poetess Ines de la Cruz, born in Mexico during the Spanish rule, and one of the most classic writers in the Spanish language; Maria Zayas y Sotomayor, a novelist of the sixteenth century; the Marchioness of Huesca, who was elected member of the Royal Academy; Maria Elguero, Maria Rosa Galvez, Feliciana Perez de Guzman, and many others whose names can be seen in the 283 volumes of books written by women, collected by the commission presided over by Her Majesty the Queen Regent, and now to be seen in the library of the Woman's Building.

It has been thought just to give in the medallions of the Spanish Pavilion a place to some of the prominent women that have died recently, and it is for that reason that the great Cuban poetess, Gemez de Avellaneda; the novelist, Fernan Caballero, and Concepcion Arenal have been given place among their sisters of past centuries.

The life of Concepcion Arenal is an illustration of what the modern Spanish woman can do. She has written books on political, sociological, and philosophical subjects that have had a great influence, and have been translated into several languages, and very fully into English.

The State recognized her talents and achievements by appointing her inspector-general of prisons and sending her as its official representative to the Penitentiary Congress at Stockholm; besides that, she has occupied a place among the most prominent men of Spain in the official commission appointed to prepare the laws of social reform, and to adjust the relations between capital and labor, and to regulate the work of women and children.

But if Spain can present in ancient and modern times as many women celebrated in all branches of human knowledge as any other nation, the true and real character of the Spanish woman is to be a home-maker, a housewife, and a mother. She contributes greatly to the prosperity and wealth of the country by her habits of order and economy and by the education she gives her children, increasing by her savings the capital of the family, making true Christians by her piety, and maintaining the national sentiment and character by the poetry and delicacy of her nature.

PRIEST'S VESTMENT. EXHIBITED BY ANGELA BAFFICO. ITALY.

The greatest ladies of the land take the lead in all the charities, following the example of the royal family. The Queen and the Infantas take the chair at weekly meetings of the boards of hospitals, asylums, and colleges, and watch in person the work of these institutions, visiting the poor, and attending to the administration of these institutions. All the ladies who have formed the commission in Madrid and the provinces are daily working for education and charity. Her Royal Highness the Infanta Isabel presides also at many of these meetings, and is at the head of " El Patronato," that has branches in all Spain for the care and education of small children.

In industry women take a very important place.

In Catalonia they work in the factories side by side with their fathers and husbands. In Valencia they control the fan and silk industry, and in the tobacco factories all the work is done by many thousands of girls in every large city. As a rule one can not say that women work in the fields in Spain. They do it in the north, where the land is very much divided; and in the other districts of Spain only during the harvest.

Unfortunately, the earnings of women are not in accordance with their work, and are very much behind those of men; but, as has been said, a national commission for social reforms has been acting in Spain for some time, and the first law presented by it to the courts was for the protection of the work of women and children.

To-day the State recognizes woman, giving her the education of the children in a great many public schools, and admitting her to the telegraph and the telephone work.

It is not possible, in the short time and the short space devoted to this paper, to give an exact idea of the character of the Spanish woman; but, apart from the exhibit in the Woman's Building— where her education and accomplishments can be studied, and where it is proved that she takes an active part in the national life— it is a good illustration of her enterprise to note what a slight examination of the catalogue shows, that there are 664 women exhibitors, nearly one-fourth of the total number of the Spanish exhibitors, and that women take part in all branches of work and thought.

THE DUCHESS OF VERAGUA.

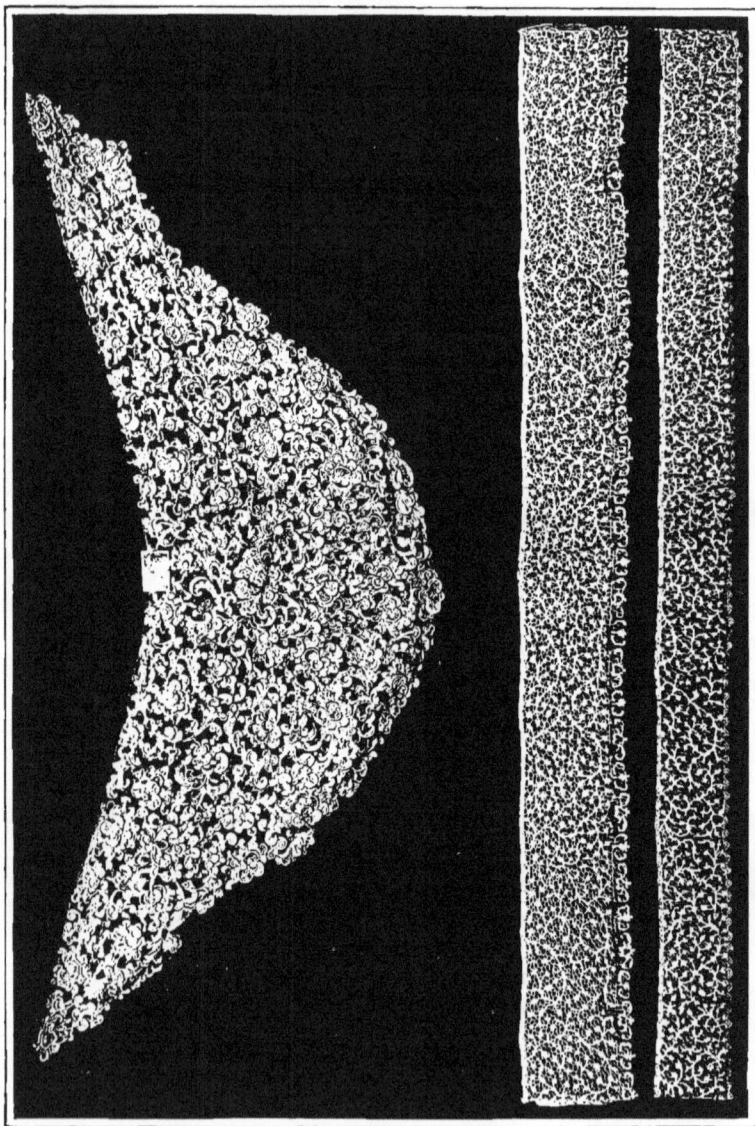

ANTIQUE RAISED VENETIAN POINT LACE. EXHIBITED BY THE COUNTESS TELFENER.
FLOUNCE VENETIAN POINT XVII CENTURY. EXHIBITED BY THE
COUNTESS DI BRAZZA. ITALY.

ITALY.

TO woman as a "ministering angel" a responsive world has rendered homage for centuries.

Of woman in her "hours of ease," of the dainty work that occupied her fingers and thoughts in the centuries prior to the invention of printing, little has been said or sung, if we except the famous Penelope, with her rather wearisome embroidery, and the equally renowned tapestry of the wife of William the Conqueror.

It is said that if all the portraits painted by Titian could be placed together, we should have an absolutely perfect historical collection of the great personages of his century.

Were it possible to make a complete collection of lace and embroidery, it would be an equally valuable pictorial history.

There exists in England a piece of lace made in the reign of Elizabeth which tells the story of the Spanish Armada; the angry waves are as billowy as lace can make them, and the discomfited galleys are historically interesting in outline.

It is a pleasant thought that the art of lace-making, like the early pictures of Cimabue and Giotto, was called into being and encouraged by the religious spirit of the age. Pleasant, because the old masters were "teachers of men," and, before the invention of printing, sought to bring holy thoughts to men's minds by the power of their art; indeed the Italian peasant still calls lace "nuns' work."

Lace is, however, of far more ancient origin. Recent discoveries have proved beyond a doubt that the making of lace was practiced by the Lake Dwellers; fragments of drawn work have also been found in Etruscan tombs and wrapped about Egyptian mummies, and specimens come as well from the savage tribes of Africa; in fact, wherever woman has made a home the needle has told its story. The story may be woven in the costly meshes known as *Argentan* or *Alençon*, or in the less complicated "points" of *Brussels*, *Mechlin*, and *Venice*, but to the thoughtful, each piece of lace is the history of a portion of a woman's life.

In Venice a sailor once brought his lady-love a sprig of coral

from distant seas, and she, sitting dreamily, in his absence, copied
the delicate branches in lace, and thus produced one of the love-
liest of Venetian designs.

Venetian lace resembles the foam of the Adriatic as the waves
break on the Lido. Just as her famous glass has caught in its iridescent splendor the matchless delicacy of her sunsets over the
lagoons, so her point laces express in their lightness and variety
the unique charm of the place. Compare them, for instance, with
the Flemish laces, dear stolid Antwerp with her "pot lace" that is

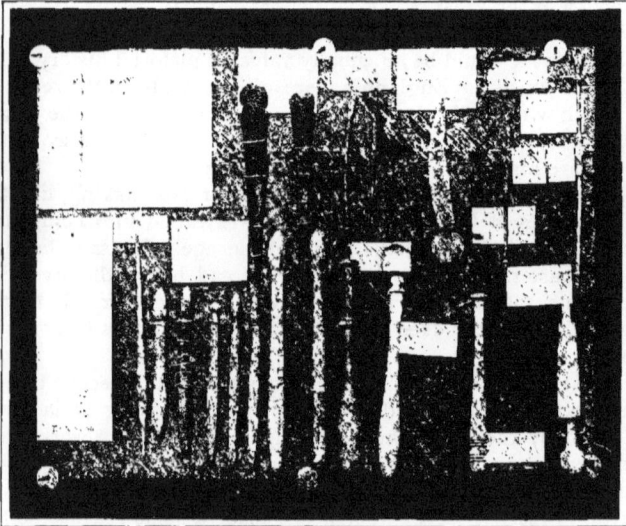

COLLECTION OF LACE NEEDLES AND BOBBINS.
EXHIBITED BY THE COMMITTEE OF ITALIAN LADIES.

so in request by old ladies for their caps! The flower-pot is all
that is left of a once charming design of the annunciation; the
graceful figures of the Virgin and of the angel Gabriel have dis-
appeared, but the lily in its pot on the window-sill has survived.

In the splendor-loving days of France, girls with little baskets
of lace went about the streets of Paris selling dainty jabots and
collars, as flower-girls sell their wares nowadays.

The prejudices against this most feminine industry are happily dissipating before the well-authenticated statistics concerning
the physical and moral well-being of the lace-workers of this

BAPTISMAL VEIL OF QUEEN CAROLINE OF NAPLES.
EXHIBITED BY MARCHIONESS MAZZECORATI.
RED SATIN EMBROIDERED COVER. VENICE, XV CENTURY.
EXHIBITED BY COUNTESS DI BRAZZA.
JABOT OF JEROME BONAPARTE. KING OF WESTPHALIA.
FLOUNCE OF THE QUEEN OF WESTPHALIA. EXHIBITED BY COUNTESS DI PAPADOPOLI.
ITALY.

century. (I give precedence to the word physical, considering the moral largely dependent upon it.)

In the Woman's Building at the Columbian Exposition the history of lace, from prehistoric times to the most perfect specimens of the modern school of Burano, is illustrated in a collection of great interest, including the priceless antique laces graciously lent by Her Majesty the Queen of Italy.

There is a complete set of antique bobbins of bone, terra cotta, bronze, and ivory, and the figure of a woman with her pillow of unfinished lace to illustrate the process.

The revival of the lace industry has resulted all over Italy in the greatest benefit to the peasantry, the success of which is greatly owing to the indefatigable energy of an American, Cora Slocomb, Countess di Brazzá, whose untiring example has inspired many others.

It is customary to think of Italy as a country that has had her day. No mistake is greater. Bologna, the quaint old university town, with her leaning towers, her picturesque arcaded streets, and medieval palaces, is still mentally alive, and has kept awake during the long sleep of centuries in which some of the nations lay unconscious.

There are at present fifteen women students in the university, the most learned of whom is a Signorina Catani of Imola, twenty-eight years of age, who has been a student there for nine years, and is now assistant to Professor Tizzoni in "general pathology." She is a worthy successor to the famous Bolognese women of the past who occupied the chairs of philosophy, jurisprudence, and medicine.

Among these, as early as the twelfth century, the famous Novella lectured upon philosophy. Her beauty equaled her learning, so that she was obliged to lecture behind a veil in order not to endanger the peace of mind of the sterner sex!

In the thirteenth century Bettisia Gozzadini was a "reader of law" in the university. Her portrait is in Bologna, a truly lovely head, an ideal Portia!

Laura Bassi, wife of Professor Verati, was professor of philosophy, and equally learned in mathematics and physics. She was a member of the Academy of Bologna, and devoted her leisure to writing poetry.

The pride of Bologna, the woman whom the university justly delights to honor, is Anna Manzolini, who, 115 years ago, filled the chair of anatomy at the university. Her wonderful anatomical reproductions in wax, as well as the portrait busts of herself and her husband which she modeled, are still to be seen there. She was made an honorary member of all the scientific and literary academies of Europe, and offered professorships in Milan, London, and St. Petersburg, but she never left Bologna.

The famous Clotilde Tambroni filled the Greek professorship at the university at the beginning of this century, and is naïvely described by her Italian biographer as " singularly modest in voice,

MACRAME TOWELS.
MODERN AND ANCIENT DESIGNS. THE EVOLUTION OF MACRAME FROM SIMPLE KNOTS TO FINE LACE. ITALY.

gestures, and dress, *even at the height of her glory.*" The future of Italy is as full of hope as her past is rich in example, and under the stimulating influence of Margherita di Savoia, not merely "Queen of Italy," but intellectually the highest lady in the land, the future of woman grows daily brighter

EVA MARIOTTI.

EMBROIDERY. CHARLOTTE GEORGEVILLE. FRANCE.

WOMAN'S POSITION IN THE SPANISH-AMERICAN STATES.

IN order to obtain a correct appreciation of the present condition of the Spanish-American woman it will be necessary to bear in mind the influence exerted by many circumstances appertaining to ancient times, as well as the action of more recent and immediate causes.

The bulk of the Spanish-American population is mainly composed of two elements: First, the descendants of the Spanish conquerors. Second, the native Indian races of Central and South America. The first one, although far inferior in numbers, has always been and continues to be the only ruling power in all the states.

These two elements brought into contact during four centuries have never become assimilated to any considerable extent. It might be said that they have rather kept themselves at a distance from each other, so that the overwhelming majority still remains a pure-blooded Indian, while only a small portion of it has become mixed with the Spanish race.

But even this partial union of those elements could not produce any substantial change in the position of woman in the Spanish-American colonies. She had always lived surrounded by a similar atmosphere and placed under similar circumstances in Spanish as well as in Indian civilization, her field of action never extending beyond the narrow limits of the family and of religious institutions, the church, convent, etc. In public life she was totally absent, absolutely ignored, as if she could not have any political significance whatever. Beyond the walls of the family dwellings she could become nothing but a Spanish nun or an Indian vestal.

The form of government was essentially monarchical and theocratic in Spain, as it was in Indian countries. The *divine right* of kings was the same in both; and, as a natural consequence, in the course of several centuries the most exclusive religious sentiment became the main characteristic of the population. It must be added that the secular war in which Spain fought for national

PARIS VASE—MEDALLION IN POLYCHROME PAINTING ON GRAY ENAMEL.
MME. E. APOIL. FRANCE.

independence and religious creed made a single block of these two principles, and fused patriotic feeling and the Catholic faith to such a degree that they became one and the same thought and aspiration in every part of that warlike and proud nation. Such is the mold in which Spanish-American character was shaped.

BAS RELIEF—"OPHELIA." SARAH BERNHARDT. FRANCE.

The effects of this cause were, of course, much deeper in woman's character, owing to her natural sensibility, her instinctive religious tendency, and the docility with which she adapts herself to the influences prevailing in her home. Being inexorably excluded from all participation in political or public life, her patriotic

18

"POINT COUPÉ." MADE BY PEASANT WOMEN OF ZEELAND. LENT BY THE PRINCESS ROYAL LOUISE OF DENMARK, NÉE PRINCESS OF SWEDEN AND NORWAY.

feeling remained latent, the whole of her activity being thus completely absorbed by her domestic duties and religious worship.

Laws, traditions, and habits worked together in restraining to an excessive degree the freedom and power of woman, even in the narrow field of her strictly private life. Her existence from beginning to end passed in passive submission to the authority and will of her *lord and master;* and in spite of the chivalrous character of the Spaniard, the companion of his life was no better than any of her oriental ancestors, an imprisoned or enslaved beauty, deprived of all the blessings and advantages of education and learning.

Yet it is doubtful if there are more intelligent or better endowed women in any region of the earth. Her quick comprehension, her bright imagination, her artistic propensities, her truly wonderful precocity, and even her impulsive and passionate character, will evidently mark in the course of time the transformation of this brilliant and fascinating *spoiled child* into the noblest type of woman, shining amidst the elements of national and universal progress. I am conscious of not overestimating the richness of her nature when I affirm that there is no heroic self-abnegation, no sublime ideal, no delicate refinement, no degree of moral courage to which she can not rise.

The war for the emancipation of the Spanish colonies of America was the first shock that awakened the Spanish-American woman from her slumbers, and opened to her astonished eyes a new and brilliant horizon. She was everywhere an enthusiastic agent and a devoted champion of the independent party, carrying her action so far that on several occasions the Spanish military executions reddened with her blood the soil she labored to liberate.

During the protracted period of internal convulsion and civil war that preceded the organization and present state of the Spanish-American republics, the influence of woman was frequently felt in prominent events of political life. She had no right granted by law to interfere with such matters, but she deemed her right to be sufficiently justified by her own self-sacrifice in the war for independence. Her action was in many instances an efficient force that brought about the final solution, and gave rise to deep changes—nay, to the very existence of new governments.

In later years new laws have swept away some of the most powerful obstacles opposed by ancient legislation to the improvement of woman's position in private and public life. The barrier of religious intolerance was partially demolished in several of the new republics, and the free access of foreign immigration to their respective territories produced a large number of inter-marriages and of new homes where an enlightened and liberal spirit prevails.

Public and private education began to spread in the upper classes of the young nations, although for the most part it still

PAINTING "THE OLD MAN'S SOUP." MME. ARTHUR ARNOULD. FRANCE.

remained in the hands of sectarian teachers and religious institutions. But in the last score of years a most considerable progress has been accomplished by the united action of governments and private individuals in the principal Spanish-American states.

It is with the deepest feeling of joy and pride that I call attention to the influence of our sex in this great evolution. Nearly all the schools for girls are actually placed under the control of female teachers; normal schools for women are amply supported or protected by the national authorities; large and beautiful buildings, that in some cities are true palaces, have been erected for educational purposes; and hundreds of foreign professors are being continually brought from their native countries to the hospitable and promising homes of Spanish America.

The majority of female teachers are native girls, who have obtained reliable credentials ; and it can be confidently asserted that there will be in the future no lack or deficiency in the supply of intelligent direction for all public schools.

This has been the first authorized step of the Spanish-American woman's career beyond the limits of domestic life. Another important movement, attained by a strength of will and moral courage of which no one unacquainted with Spanish countries can even form an idea, is the admission lately granted to female students to the curriculum of the regular universities.

To duly appreciate this success it will be necessary to remember certain circumstances peculiar to several of the Spanish-American countries which formed an almost impassable barrier against so great an innovation. For many generations woman had been regarded in every Spanish community as a being deprived by nature of every condition of mind and character fit for any sober or serious purpose. She could be but a comfort and an ornament in the home of her proud and indolent master. On the other hand, with the exception of legal and military affairs, labor in whatever form was sincerely despised by the nobility, or governing class, of the country. Even such professions as medicine, architecture, and engineering (as it existed at the time) were carried on by individuals of the colored race, and not infrequently by slaves. Contempt for labor had thus become in all classes of society a habit, an instinct, a deeply rooted feeling, that even to this day shows its vitality in spite of foreign intercourse and advanced education. Daily experience, with its eloquent teachings, has to a certain extent undermined that ancient prejudice. Still, what remains of the old spirit is enough to shake the most resolute courage.

It might therefore be said in all truth that the Spanish-American woman has carried the position by storm, and she may justly be proud of her new victory.

Although in very limited numbers, there are at present lawyers, physicians, dentists, midwives of the female sex, who sustain a decorous position among their male colleagues.

The expansive force of her natural talent has found a broad field besides in almost every branch of art and literature—drawing, painting, music, poetry, romance afford a pleasant employment for the leisure hours of the educated woman, and in many instances have given her a reputation which extends beyond the boundaries of her native country. Several women rank as high in Spanish literature, especially in poetry, as some of the old classic writers, and stand almost on a level with the very best poets of the present day.

Even the political press begins to feel the influence of woman, there being already a few daily or periodical newspapers edited by women, and devoted to the interest of some political organization. It is unnecessary to add that they are always enthusiastic defenders of woman's rights.

It must not be forgotten that the foregoing remarks concern only a small class of women placed in the most favorable circumstances, and that even among them literary and artistic labor are not professional. Still, there is no doubt that before long it will become as useful and productive as any career opened to the activity of our sex.

The number of girls and women belonging to the middle class (and they are generally more or less educated) who find in their own exertions some means of support is very limited indeed. In the great majority of cases they remain a burden to their parents, their husbands, or some other male members of the family; and, in spite of their natural disinterestedness, girls are sometimes induced to accept a marriage by necessity rather than by choice.

This truly deplorable condition of affairs can not be suddenly changed, as it is a natural effect of the peculiar organization of Spanish society. The Spaniard, and, still more, his American descendant, deems himself disgraced, dishonored, if it is known that his wife, his daughter, or his sister works for her living, or for the improvement of her home. Such a prejudice and false pride could only have arisen in the period of fantastic wealth, when almost everybody lived rich and happy in the Spanish colonies without the trouble of any personal labor, for all the work was carried on by slaves. That immense wealth passed away long ago, yet the old proud feeling still remains. How long will it last?

Let us hope that more frequent intercourse with foreign peoples, together with the necessity of securing domestic happiness by providing young girls with elements of self-support, so as to make them the companions and helpmates, not the servile attendants, of their husbands, will soon do away with that unnatural inactivity of so many intelligent and educated women.

With the exception of some of the post office, telephone, and telegraphic offices, there is not a single official bureau where women are regularly employed; and besides certain lines of tramways in a few cities, and occasionally in a small number of stores and shops, they are never seen anywhere in the vast field of public or private activity.

To close the series of these brief notes, I submit two very significant facts, viz.: First, the spirit of association for serious and useful purposes, lately initiated among the Spanish-American women and attaining every day more remarkable proportions. Second, the ever-increasing circulation of literary and scientific books and periodicals among the women of the principal cities in almost every one of those States.

It is the moral duty, as well as the practical interest, of the North American people to extend to the young and promising nations of Spanish-America the influence of their modern institutions, and the liberal and progressive spirit which is advancing the cause of woman; and very particularly the atmosphere of freedom and encouragement that surrounds the life of our sex in the North. No field richer in

EMBOSSED COPPERS.
ROSALIE JUEL. SWEDEN.

promise can be opened to their energies than the more complete social emancipation of the Spanish-American woman—a blessing of which she has proved to be worthy in every respect—and that no nation could as easily as yours grant to these sympathetic and benevolent homes. It seems to me an axiomatic truth that to complete the personality of woman in the domestic and social life is to secure her legitimate influence and civilizing power in the general evolution of mankind.

MATILDE G. DE MIRO QUESADA.

RUINS OF YUCATAN. THE LABNA PORTAL, ETC. REPRODUCED IN STAFF, UNDER DIRECTIONS OF PROF. PUTNAM.

WATER COLOR PORTRAIT OF HER MAJESTY THE EMPRESS OF RUSSIA.
MLLE. KRANESKOL.

VIEW OF THE MAIN BASIN, LOOKING NORTH.

RUSSIA.

O UT of the distant gloom of the earliest period of our history a woman's name shines among the beams that lightened the dawn of Christianity.

Princess Olga, widow of Prince Igor, at the beginning of the tenth century, went to Byzantium to be baptized in the Christian faith. During the minority of her son Sviatoslav, she ruled her land and its chief town, Kieff. The chronicles never use her name without the apellation of "most wise." The church has canonized her.

When, in the year 989, her grandson, Prince Vladimir, was on the point of making the choice of one of the Christian creeds for himself and his people, he said: "Our grandmother Olga, who was the wisest woman, was baptized in Greece," and this settled it. He was married to the Byzantine Princess Ann, sister of the emperors Constantine and Basil. In the second half of the eleventh century two Russian princesses, daughters of Yaroslar, were Queen of France and Queen of Sweden. In the course of later history, names of women but seldom appear, for the way of living prohibited them from taking any prominent part in social life. They lived in a separate part of the house—so often mentioned in songs and poetry, the " Terem" (the "ladies' high bower " of English poems)—and they were but very seldom allowed to come into men's society. The Tartar yoke, that lasted from 1224-1480, and had such a disastrous influence on the development of our civilization, in keeping us back for over two centuries, must be taken in consideration when speaking of the women at this period. The reign of Peter the Great is generally considered as the epoch of a complete change in the Russian woman's social position, but a gradual advance toward it can be followed up for a long time before. In the fifteenth century, after the fall of Constantinople, John III., Grand Duke of Moscow, married the Byzantine Princess Sophia Paleologue (hence the Byzantine eagle adopted as the Russian coat-of-arms); from this time several names of women appear in history.

Though they are not in immediate connection with any special

PEN AND INK SKETCH—LANDSCAPE. BY THE PRINCESS IMIRETINSKY. RUSSIA.

event, they must be mentioned on account of the influence they had on their surroundings. In the beginning of the sixteenth century the handsome and intelligent Helen Glinsky was known for the power she had over her husband, Grand Duke Vassili, father of John IV. A happy period in the reign of this cruel monarch, surnamed "The Terrible," is due to the influence of Anastasia Romanovna, one of his seven wives. His son Theodor's wife, Jrina Godounova, was extolled by all foreign travelers and ambassadors who came to Moscow, for her charms and beauty and her wise and loving dealings with her husband, who lacked strength both in mind and body.

In the second half of the seventeenth century, the family of the boyar Artamon Matveieff was one of the most cultivated in Moscow. In this house Tsar Alexis (the second of the present reigning family of Romanoffs), who was a widower at this time, met the young Nathalie Kirilovna Narishkine, his host's ward. The handsome girl captivated the sovereign's heart, became his wife, and mother of Peter the Great.

By his first wife Alexis had a daughter who was certainly one of the most remarkable figures of her time. She was intelligent and devoted to literature, encouraged dramatic art, and composed some tragedies, which unfortunately are lost. During the minority of her brothers, John and Peter, the Princess Sophia ruled the kingdom in their name. Foreign ambassadors who were received in state at the Muscovite court were strongly impressed by the sight of two royal boys sitting on a double-seated throne, and obeying the whisper of a female voice coming from behind a curtain. Her political wisdom and popularity among the people and the army were such that Peter, at a later period, considered her of such dangerous importance that she was captured, relegated to a monastery, and forced to take the veil.

The first years of the last century mark the turning-point in our women's social life. Among the innovations that Peter the Great imposed on the society of the newly rising St. Petersburg were the so-called "assemblies," or evening parties, held at court, where ladies were *obliged* to be present, much to the annoyance of the grumbling partisans of "olden times." After Peter the Great's death, in 1725, his widow, Catharine I., was the first of a series of women who sat on the imperial throne, interrupted only by the short reigns of Peter II. and Peter III. These empresses were Ann, Duchess of Courland, Peter the Great's niece; Elizabeth, his daughter; and lastly, Catharine II. the Great.

ANCIENT RUSSIAN HEAD-GEAR. EXHIBITED BY MME. SCHABELSKOI. RUSSIA.

A mention is due of the name of the famous friend of the latter, the Princess Dashkoff, president of the Academy of Science in St. Petersburg. Of great culture and learning, she was known as well abroad as in Russia. She had traveled much, and carried on a large correspondence with scientific men. Her interesting memoirs, written in French, form a volume of the " Prince Worontzoff's archives."

The first female educational institutions date from the reign of Catharine the Great. Seminaries for girls of noble families were founded, the education given being somewhat like the French convent education.

Empress Maria Theodorovna, wife of Paul I., continued the same work. With untiring and never-failing love she encouraged all private and official activity in the field of education and charity. The number of seminaries, schools, hospitals, homes, etc., opened under her high patronage grew to such an extent that after her death it was considered necessary to found a special ministry for their management; they formed the "Institutions of Empress Maria," and have been ever since the object of special care to all our empresses.

In the middle of this century rises a brilliant name indissolubly connected with all the great events of her time. The Grand Duchess Helene Pavlovna, sister-in-law of Nicholas I., was remarkable, not only for her talents, but also for the fascinating power she had of attracting around her all who were prominent in literature, art, science, and politics. The musical and literary gatherings in the "Palais Michel" were famous. She founded and was the first president of the St. Petersburg Musical Conservatory. Emperor Alexander II. highly appreciated her intelligence, and she was one of his nearest counselors in the great act of the emancipation of serfs. In her charity and educational activity, which was great, she was efficiently assisted by Baroness Edith Rahden. The work is continued by her daughter, the Grand Duchess Catherine, who is at the head of the institutions and schools of the Patriotic Society.

This brings us to our own times, in which the great increase of feminine activity strikes us so much that I feel the insufficiency of my pen to do justice to this vast theme. So many namse shine in so many different branches that it is impossible to give here any just account of this activity. A great impulse to *education* has been given by the foundation of establishments of different types, especially gymnasiums and progymnasiums, not only in the

LANDSCAPE. PRINCESS IMRETINSKI. RUSSIA.

chief towns, but even in the small provincial places. Finally the
higher university education was opened to women in 1872, in
Petersburg, Moscow, Kieff, and Kharkoff. Private initiative and

REPRODUCTION OF CURTAIN OF THE THRONE OF THE CZARS
JEAN AND PETER, 1681.
LENT BY MME. SCHABELSKOI, MEMBER OF THE IMPERIAL RUSSIAN
HISTORICAL MUSEUM.

means have greatly contributed to the development of the inter-
mediate and higher education, such as the gymnasiums of Mme.
Taganzeff Soiounine, Princess Obolensky in Petersburg, Mme.
19

ENTRANCE TO RUSSIAN SECTION, AFTER BYZANTINE GATE XII CENTURY IN THE CHURCH OF TOURIEFF POLSKI. Oak and Fine Burnt Gold. Princess Schahkovskoy, Mme. Doubassoff, Mlle. Polienoff, Mlle. Olsonieff, the Princess Wolkowski, and others, Russia.

Perepeltine Tchepelevsky Zabeline in Moscow, and many others. Mme. Sibiriakoff (from Siberia) has done much for the advanced courses of philology and natural science in St. Petersburg, which are held in a great building provided with all resources for study-ing, such as a library, laboratories, etc.

In Science a conspicuous place belongs to the much-lamented Mme. Kovalevsky, who was a distinguished mathematician and writer. At the Astronomical Congress in Paris she took the first prize for her essay, "On the Movement of a Spherical Body round an Immutable Point." She was corresponding member of the Parisian Academy of Science, and was appointed professor of astronomy at the men's university of Stockholm. She died two years ago, not much over thirty years of age.

An honorable place belongs to Countess Ouvaroff, who, after the death of her husband, was unanimously elected president of the Archæological Society and director of the Archæological Museum at Moscow.

Medicine has been much studied by women in the last twenty years. Over seven hundred women who have been graduated as doctors are scattered over the country, being of incalculable help, especially in the southeastern part of our country, to the Moham-medan population, where women are debarred from receiving mas-culine medical help. Mesdames Sousloff, Schepeleff, Koshevaroff, Tarnovsky, and others have acquired a reputation in the medical world.

Besides this, in the smallest rural hospital every doctor is assisted by a trained professional nurse.

The institution of the *Red Cross* is of great importance, and has never failed in any occasion of war, famine, or epidemic. One of its first-rate establishments, the Community of St. Georges, in Peters-burg, is under the high patronage of the Princess Eugenie of Oldenbourg, and is directed by the Countess E. Haydn.

In Literature, in the first quarter of this century, the name of Countess Rostopchine is in that pleïad-like group of poets that group themselves around the brilliant figures of Poushkine and Lermontoff. At that epoch of intense literary life in Moscow, the salon of the Princess Zeneide Wolkonsky was the meeting place of all writers and poets. She was one of the most prominent women of her time, a distinguished musician, and very literary. She left some writings, among them an interesting correspondence with the Polish poet Mickievicz. A similar salon, renowned for its political influence and literary importance, was held in Paris by

TERRA COTTA BUST. Princess Schakowskoy. Russia.

the Russian ambassador's wife, Princess Lieven, intimate friend of Guizot and other French celebrities of this time.

Valuable memoirs have been left by Empress Catharine the Great, Empress Maria Theodovoura (not published), Countess Choiseul Gouffic, Mme. Passek, Countess Bloudoff, and the still living Mme. Shestakoff, sister of the composer Glinka.

In our days Mmes. Olga Shapiro, Eugenie Tour (Countess Salias), Krestovsky, and Kohanovsky are distinguished and very popular novelists. Many women devote their pen to literature for children and youths. The name of Mme. Novikoff (Olga Kircieff) is well known by all who are interested in political writings.

In Art women chiefly excel in its application to industry. A great deal has been done by them to raise the level of artistic taste. Mme. Couriard has the merit of being the initiator of the first women's artistic club in St. Petersburg, which she has directed for many years. Much is due in this connection to the school of the "Society of Encouragement of Arts" and its rich museum, founded by the late Grand Duchess Maria Nicolaevna, president of the Academy of Fine Arts.

As individual artists we must mention Mme. Lagoda Shishkine and Marie Bashkirtzeff, who both, unfortunately, died young. The latter has the honor of being represented in the Luxembourg picture gallery in Paris. Mlle. Polienoff is a distinguished painter and clever connoisseur. Mmes. Boehm and Beggrow-Hartmann are original painters of children scenes and portraits. As sculptors, Mme. Van-der-Hoven and Mme. Dulon.

In Music, Mme. Essipoff was pronounced by Liszt the first female pianist of our time.

In Dramatic Art, Mme. Samoiloff has left a great name, and Mmes. Fedotoff and Yermoloff are the ornaments of the Moscow Dramatic Theater at this moment.

The last few years have brought up quite a new kind of activity that consists in helping, encouraging, and directing the rural industries of peasant women. Hand-made laces, embroideries, rugs, carpets, spinning, weaving, knitting, etc., have all been taken under their patronage by lady land-owners in their country places. Schools, museums, stores, and bazars have been arranged in the largest towns, so as to make these products known, and facilitate their sale.

Mme. A. Narishkine in the province of Tamboff, Mme. G. Narishkine, Mme. Davidoff, Mme. Mamontoff near Moscow, Princess Ouroussoff in Toula, and many others devote their time, money, and energy toward enlarging and spreading these industries.

ANCIENT RUSSIAN HEAD-GEAR. EXHIBITED BY MME. SCHABELSKOI, RUSSIA.

Mme. Schabelskoy's most wonderful and rare collection of Russian woman's ancient work is not yet open to the public, but is of greatest scientific importance as saving from oblivion old patterns and designs.

Of Charity I find it unnecessary to speak, for in Russia, as everywhere else, woman has always considered it her special field.

Something of the status of Russian woman can be learned from the following details: She inherits (when there is no special testament) the fourteenth part of her father's and seventh part of her husband's fortune. In marrying she keeps all rights of possession in complete equality with the man. Land-owning gives her all the same privileges, such as voting (not personally, but by proxy) in the provincial and municipal elections.

Thus we see that Russian woman takes a great part in the social and political life of her country; and that whichever way man wishes to direct his activity, woman will always stand by him with helping and encouraging hand.

Our national literature that has always truly represented Russian life in all its depths and variety has made of the Russian woman a beloved and inexhaustible subject. Its masterpieces offer highest examples of feminine character; the type has been immortalized by the pen of such men as Poushkine, Tolstoy, Tourgueneff, Gontcharoff, and Russian women can be proud of the tribute that *fiction* pays to *reality*.

PRINCESS M. SCHAHOVSKOY.

Attention is called to the beautiful entrance of the Russian section. This is a reproduction of a Byzantine gate of the twelfth century, in the famous church of Tourieff Polski. It is made of oak, and is a triumph of fine joiner's work, not one nail being used. The quaint and delicate design is produced by a method invented by the Princess Schakowskoy. The surface of the wood is overlaid with real gold-leaf, from which the design is burnt out. The color produced by the gold sinking into the wood is very rich and unique. We are glad to learn that this piece of work, which was designed and made by Russian women, may be bought and retained in our country at the close of the Fair.—ED.

BUREAU OF PUBLIC COMFORT.

SANCTA BRIGITTA

PAINTED GLASS WINDOW. CECILIA BOKLUND. SWEDEN.

BIRD'S-EYE VIEW FROM THE FERRIS WHEEL, LOOKING EAST.

T HE love of knowledge is a distinguishing feature in the character of Swedes.

The Swedish woman has not manifested less love of knowledge than is attributed to her nation.

A certain amount of school education has for centuries been considered necessary to woman, and, especially in the middle of this century, claims arose for a higher standard in her education.

ALTAR PIECE — ROMANESQUE STYLE.
DESIGNED BY A. BRANTING; "FRIENDS OF HANDIWORK." SWEDEN.

The royal academies of music and fine arts, the training schools for sloid and gymnastics were opened to women, and they have the same rights as men for studying at the universities.

As teachers, principals of schools, members of school boards, lady inspectors, authors in pedagogics, etc., women have attained an influence which is steadily increasing.

The endeavors to raise the standard of manual work has called forth the efforts of many Swedish women. Misses Eva Rodhe and Hulda Lundin have developed the excellent systems of sloid. The

PAINTED SCREEN — IMITATION GOBELIN. ANNA BOBERG, SWEDEN.

latter exhibits a series of models in the Swedish section of the
Woman's Building, where is also to be seen a very fine collection
of fancy works from the Society of Art Handiwork, and from
Misses Giobel, Kulle, Zickerman, Ahrberg, Randel, Ingelotz, and
others.

This society has in a high degree refined the taste and raised

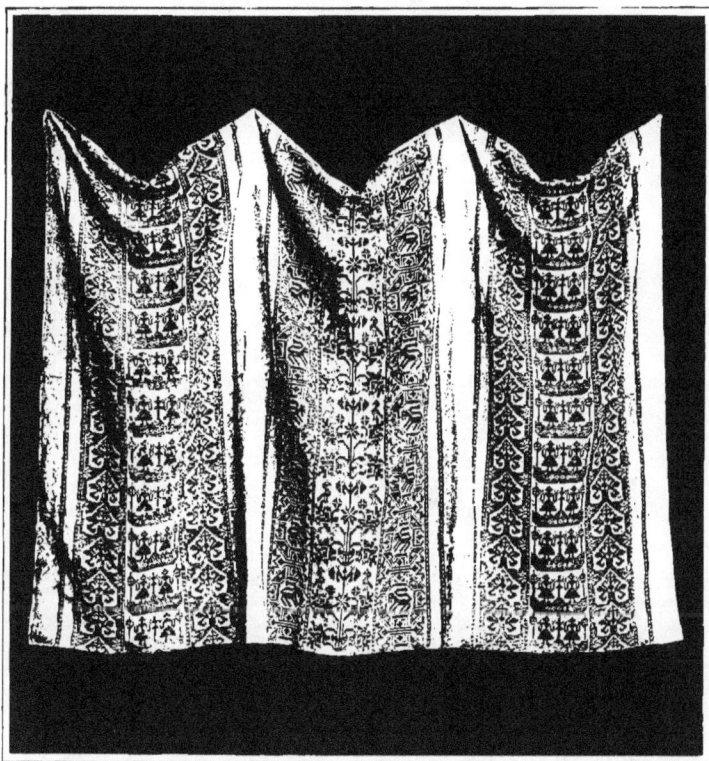

LINEN CHATTADUK WALL HANGING. MME. CILLUF ALSSON, SCANIA. SWEDEN.

the standard of woman's industrial work. It has adapted old
designs and encouraged the original Swedish lace-work, tapestry,
and weaving, and by doing so has preserved for the country a
national industrial art which might otherwise have been entirely
lost.

We find in this section some fine etched glass by Mrs. Petterson, and a cistern in embossed copper by Mrs. Juel.

TAPESTRY.   BENGKA OLSSON.   SWEDEN.

An interesting medal exhibit is given by Lea Ahlborn, who is connected with the royal mint, and designs medals for the government.

The portrait of the Queen of Sweden and Norway, patroness of the Swedish Ladies Committee to the World's Columbian Exposition, hangs on the wall of the booth, and is surrounded by tapestries.

In the library of the building are 130 volumes by the most eminent authors, from which we cite the names of Sta Briggita, Fredrika Bremer, Leffler-Caianello, Benedictson, Olivecrona, Adlersparre, Roos, and others.

Several portraits have been hung in Assembly Hall. Among them are pictures of Jenny Lind, Christine Nilsson, Fredrika Bremer, and Sta Briggita.

A stand holds music written by Mrs. Netzel, Misses Aulin, Andrée, and Munktell.

A beautiful portfolio and an album in embossed leather, by Miss Gisberg, incloses photographs and biographies of eminent musicians and authors of the present time.

A large number of ladies have studied at the Academy of Fine Arts, and many female names have been prominent among the painters of the last decades.

Among the exhibitors in the Swedish Section of Fine Arts, we find Mrs. Pauli, Mrs. Chadwick, Misses Bonnier, Schultzenheim, Keyser, and Jolin, and in the Swedish pavilion, water-colors by Miss Anna Palm.

As we have tried to show by the above, the Swedish woman takes a great interest and an active part in the great works of culture,

LARGE GOBLET OF ETCHED GLASS.
HILDA PETTERSON. SWEDEN.

and it was, therefore, with much pleasure she received the invitation from her American sister, the most accomplished woman of our time, to take part in the Columbian Exposition.

THORBORG RAPPE.

COSTUME OF A "HEDEBIPOGE"—PEASANT WOMAN OF ZEELAND, DENMARK.

DENMARK.

LAND of the North, of short somber days and long gloomy nights! If during half the year nature seems to chastise your people with one hand, she blesses them with the other. The long winter evenings must perforce be spent at the fireside:

CUSHION AND WORKCASE.
Formerly Given by a Lover to His Betrothed; from the Island of Amager.
EXHIBITED BY MME. HOLMBLAD, NEE SCHACK. DENMARK.

thus a love of home is developed, and with it a cultivation of those homely gifts which transform the cottage hearth into a school of domestic art.

20 (305)

From time immemorial the peasants have gathered around
their firesides in the long winter evenings, the men carving
wood or mending their nets, the women busy with their looms and

OIL PAINTING—FLOWERS.
BY QUEEN LOUISE OF DENMARK, NEE PRINCESS OF HESSE. DENMARK.

embroidery, while the village story-teller recites tales of war, of
love, and of chivalry. In the National Museum at Copenhagen
and in many Danish houses we find mementos of those evenings

of long ago. In making a selection for the exhibit of work to be
sent to the Woman's Building at Chicago, it has been thought best
to give, as it were, a retrospective glance at the work of the Danish
women in the past, as their modern industries are fully represented
by Denmark's general exhibit.

OLD SILK PETTICOAT.
In the Possession of the d'Arenstorff Family for Two Hundred Years
EXHIBITED BY MME. VALLO, NÉE D'ARENSTORFF. DENMARK.

The most ancient article in the collection is a superb petticoat,
embroidered by hand, belonging to Madame Wallo, *née* d'Arenstorff, which has been in her family since the seventeenth century.
A baptismal robe is remarkable for the daintiness of the stitchery;
the baby doll, in state swaddling-clothes, and the bridal veil are

worthy of notice. The heavy brocades, embroidered linen, and
peasant costumes are all characteristic and interesting. One rare
and beautiful piece of work, a sewing cushion, has a certain
romantic interest; it is the gift of a lover to his betrothed, and sig-
nifies that the time to prepare the trousseau has come.

The vinaigrettes and antique perfumery bottles exhibited are
remarkable for the number and variety of their designs.

CARVED WOOD FRAME. MLLE. HAWKINS. DENMARK.

The fichus in silk embroidery of H. R. H. the princess royal
form the beautiful head-dress and mantle of the costume worn by
the peasants on the Island of L'Amerger.

A crowning interest in the exhibit is found in the painting of
roses and lilies by Her Majesty Queen Louise; artistic embroidery
and illuminated parchment by the princess royal of Denmark;
three water-colors by Her Royal Highness Princess Woldersov, and
the exquisite ebony frame designed and executed by Miss Hawkins
in the highest style of workmanship.

MME. D'OXHOLM.

SCARCELY sixty years have passed since Greece regained her liberty. During the servile period of her history the status of women was alike precarious and miserable. Man was indeed a slave; but woman was the slave of a slave. So ancient tradition decreed, which even to-day underlies the manners of the Greeks, strengthened by Mussulman influences which have left their impress upon the subjugated generations.

Even now, in the country and the smaller provincial towns, woman is regarded as an inferior being. In the enumeration of his children, the father ignores the females. Women are not privileged to sit at meat with guests; while in the rural districts they are subjected to the severest labors, cultivating the soil and bowing beneath the weight of grievous burdens of wood and water, brought from a distance. In the villages they remain in-doors, and are seldom seen abroad. In the evening they sit upon their balconies, and on Sunday they offer their prayers within the space reserved for them in the sanctuary. An active participation in affairs is the prerogative of men only, who read the papers, learn the condition of the markets, and make all the purchases for the household.

This rigor is somewhat relaxed in the larger cities, where greater liberty and consideration are accorded to women. Yet even here their tasks are limited to the education of children and the management of domestic affairs. They have no special occupation, no industry to follow, unless it be that of a servant or governess, or perhaps occasionally the trade of a seamstress or *modiste*, or an operative in one of the few cotton or silk factories.

This degraded condition of Greek women is readily understood, since Greece, during the centuries preceding her proclamation of independence, subject to Turkish rule, and, as it were, isolated from the rest of the world, failed to participate in the great movement of the Renaissance which awakened the civilization of Europe. Roused by her heroic struggle for liberty, she at last recovered the position lost in submission to the yoke of foreign invasion; yet rising from the ruins of her glory, it was necessary, before

turning attention to the social state of her women, to cultivate the
wasted soil, rebuild her cities and towns, and perfect the government. To these ends have the Greek government and citizens
labored incessantly, even to this day.

EMBROIDERED SILK CUSHION.
DESIGNED BY AGNES BRANTING; EXHIBITED BY "THE FRIENDS OF HANDIWORK." SWEDEN.

Meanwhile, private enterprise has sought to ameliorate the condition of women. A wealthy patriot, Arsarkis, at his own expense,
erected a women's college in Athens. Unfortunately the "Arsarkion," as it was called in honor of its founder, is not a free institution; and the same obstacle to general education attends the

establishment of three private schools in Athens, which, together with four or five others in the entire kingdom and the "Arsarkion," are the only means afforded to young women of receiving anything more than a primary education.

Under such conditions it is easy to understand that art among women is but little developed in Greece, being apparent only in weaving and embroidery. From earliest times the Greek women have spun wool, flax, and silk—as in the Homeric portraiture of Penelope—yet this industry remained comparatively uncultivated until the "Society for the Advancement of Women," under the patronage of Her Majesty Queen Olga, with Madame Skouses as president, established an industrial school for poor women.

This school, where 450 women and girls are employed, has become a source of supply, providing not only the most beautiful models and patterns of weaving and embroidery executed in the style native to the country, but the most exquisite needlework in European fashion.

Moreover, the institution is a philanthropic one, furnishing work for 450 needy women, giving them elementary instruction and providing dinners at a cost of from two to four cents. All labor is piece-work, at prices determined by the superintendent of the society, and all the articles sent to the Exposition are the product of the above institution in Athens.

In the Hellenic provinces women execute similar work. At Tripoli and Leonidi, in the Peloponnesus, and at Arachona and Atlanta, in Locris, carpets are woven; at Kalamata, in Messenia, and at Aghia and Ambelakia, in Thessaly, silk-stuffs are made; at Tripoli, Argos, Missolonghi, and Levadia cotton goods are manufactured; and at Tyrnavo, in Thessaly, printed cottons are prepared. Besides these manufactures, like fabrics are made in almost every home, and in a large proportion of houses we find a loom.

It is in the execution of these textile articles that the taste of the Greek women is displayed. Their work possesses, moreover, a quality of original design and of simplicity, without sacrifice of delicate detail, which augurs favorably for the future development of women's industries in Greece.

MADAME QUELLENEC.

OIL PAINTING—"AUTUMN EVENING." E. BEERNART. BELGIUM.

BELGIUM.

THE exhibit made by Belgium in the Woman's Building was collected by a committee under the patronage of Her Majesty the Queen of the Belgians. The honorary president, the Countess of Flanders, is well known not only as a patron of the arts and industries of women, but as a painter herself. The president, Mme. de Denterghen, is maid of honor to the Queen; the other officers and members of the committee are all women whose high positions have enabled them to gather together the very valuable collection which is installed in that section of the Woman's Building devoted to Belgium. The arrangement of the space is very charming. Passing under some finely wrought hangings, the work and gift of Belgian working-women, the visitor finds himself in a salon, hung with good pictures, and filled with cases containing fine examples of china-painting, fan-painting and mounting, miniatures, embroideries, and laces. The best known of the contemporaneous women painters, Mme. Ronner, is represented by one of her inimitable paintings of a group of cats, which hangs in the Hall of Honor. Other people have painted cats, but Mme. Ronner stands to-day as the most famous cat painter in the world. She has studied the habits and character of her favorite animal, and understands cat and kitten nature thoroughly. The standard of excellence of the painters represented is very high; out of the twenty artists who exhibit their work in the Woman's Building, eleven have taken honors at other important exhibitions. A group of etchings by the Countess of Flanders has received much well-merited praise, while the single small piece of sculpture, a plow-horse, by the Comtesse d'Espiennes, makes the visitor wish to see more of her strong, sympathetic work. Some excellent examples of china-painting are exhibited by the School of the Rue de Marais at Brussels. The ecclesiastic embroideries of Mlle. Dennis are worthy of attention, and the white embroideries of Mme. de Kerchove de Naeyer are masterpieces of delicate stitchery.

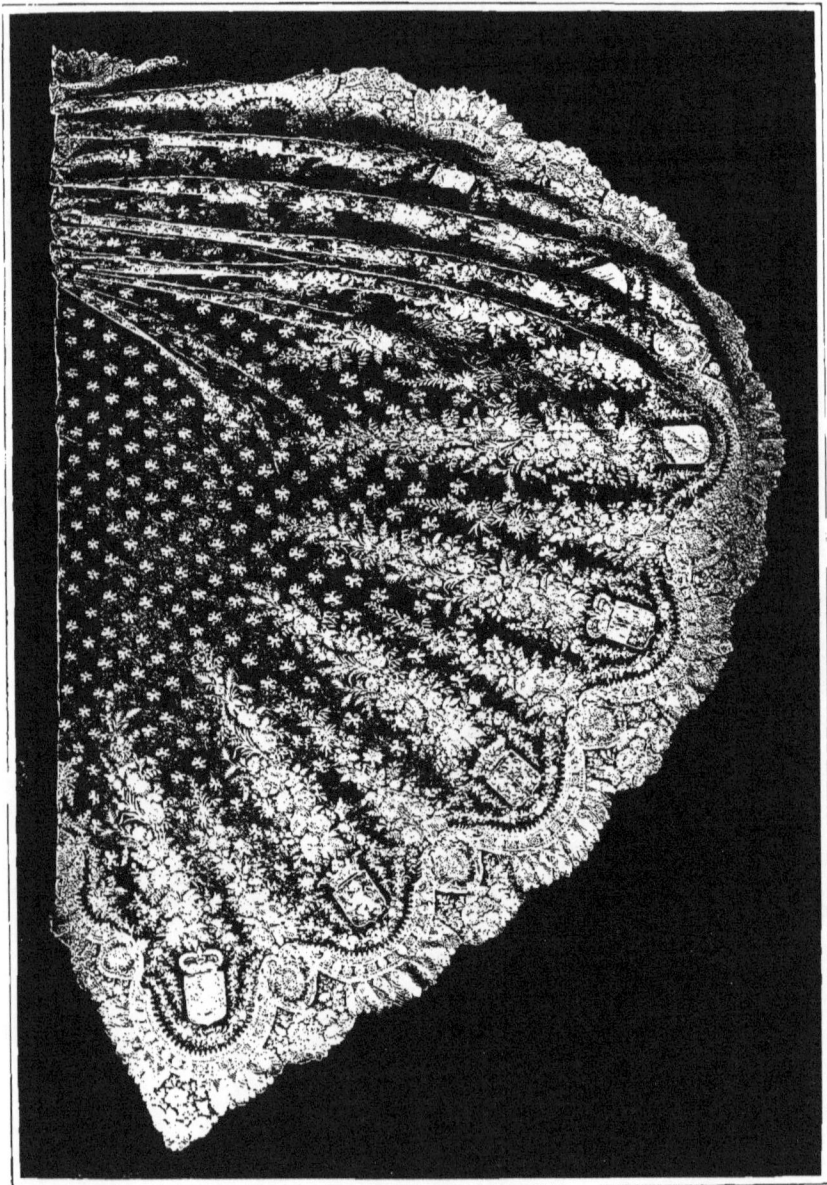

BRUSSELS DRESS, APPLIQUÉ ON REAL NET. PROPERTY OF HER MAJESTY THE QUEEN OF THE BELGIANS.

The most important industry of the Belgian women is the lace-making, in which for so many years they have excelled. A good opportunity is offered to the connoisseur for the study of many rare and interesting examples of the rich laces for which Brussels, Ghent, Bruges, and so many other Flemish towns have long been famous. A dress of point d'Angleterre, lent by the Queen, is a triumph of the lace-maker's art. The coats of arms of the different Belgian provinces are wrought in the border. A veil of the Virgin, made in the last century, and lent by the Church of Saint Nicholas, has a very quaint and lovely Flemish design. Very remarkable pieces of the different styles of point lace of Malines, Valenciennes, Binche, Guipure, etc., may be studied here.

The great revival of lace-making all over Europe is very clearly illustrated at the World's Fair. We learn from the exhibits at the Woman's Building that in Ireland, Italy, France, and Russia a large amount of fine lace is being made. In Belgium the art, while it has never languished as in

PART OF LACE DRESS. EX-EMPRESS FREDERICK. GERMANY.

these other countries, has felt the same quickening impulse which in at least two countries of Europe has revived a practically extinct industry. The imitation or machine-made laces, which for some time threatened the existence of the real lace industries, have now been relegated to their proper sphere, and no more take the place of the real laces than the paste-jewel takes the place of the diamond.

Belgium is finely represented in the library, and not only by her large and interesting collection of books, but by the reports and statistics, which have been compiled with great care, and which to the student of sociology reveal much that throws light upon the condition of the people.

THE EDITOR.

CLOAK OF THE VIRGIN. BRUSSELS, XVIII CENTURY.
PROPERTY OF TREASURY OF ST. NICHOLAS CHURCH, BELGIUM.

"WHAT shall the harvest be?" This question must have occurred, sooner or later, to each of the many women who have given their time, their thought, their work, to the rearing of our woman's temple. The Algerian maiden, whose white banner was laid upon the desk on the opening day, is one of the myriads of women whose thought and sympathy have traveled to us along the slender, imperishable line of the thought railway. Our building is like the terminal station of a vast city, where the iron rails come together from the north, south, east, and west. The freight that our railway has brought is very precious, and it is because we recognize the value of what has been sent to us that the idea has arisen and gradually taken form of a granary in which to store the golden fruit, the harvest of the careful sowing and glad reaping.

FIRE SCREEN.

DESIGNED BY MARIANNE FÜRST, TEACHER IN THE VIENNA SCHOOL OF ART EMBROIDERY. MADE BY HERMINE WALTE, AUSTRIA.

The real result of the great labor can not be written in words or computed in figures. Thought outweighs brute force, wealth, art itself; and we are to-day governed by the thoughts of individ

SCREEN.

PAINTED AND EXHIBITED BY H. I. H. THE ARCHDUCHESS MARIE THERESE, AUSTRIA.

uals among peoples whose glory has become a fable. The real, permanent result of what women have done in connection with the World's Fair lies in the inscrutable future. It forms a tiny link in the great chain of human progress. Human nature, however, is a curious combination of the finite and infinite, and while we are satisfied to believe that the record of our work will be found written upon the page of to-morrow, we have a desire for something which we call real and permanent, but which is in fact perishable and evanescent. We are not content to have planted a seed which shall grow to a tree, putting forth many blossoms. We want to see at least one little sprig bloom and bear. We women are thrifty, practical beings, and it is probable that every one of us who has labored, in a little or large degree, for our building, desires that the memory of her labor shall be perpetuated in those perishable materials, brick and mortar, marble and iron.

The Kensington Museum is one of the outgrowths of the first exposition, held in London in the year 1857. This institution is the finest museum of industrial art in the world. It

LIMOGES UNDERGLAZE JAR.
E. A. RICHARDSON. UNITED STATES.

has had much to do with the improved standard of taste which has been so noticeable in England during the last half f the century. The artist and artisan study here the best examples in wood-carving, pottery, embroidery, metal-work, etc. Designing has been dignified into an art, where it was formerly a trade.

There is a wide-spread feeling that the nucleus of such a

museum now exists in the Woman's Building, and a growing desire that out of it may grow a permanent building which may serve the men and women of our country as the Kensington Museum serves the English.

It is still too early to speak definitely of this idea which is shaping itself in the public mind, but there are many who believe that the Woman's Building is the corner-stone of a new and splendid edifice; if it has been laid true, and firm, and square, the hundreds of women who have labored for it will feel that their efforts are well repaid.

In the Government Building one of the most valuable exhibits is a collection of coins of all nations and ages. It contains beautiful Greek and Roman coins, and picturesque oriental pieces of money; but in all the rich display there is not one bit of gold or silver that interests us as profoundly as the tiny bit of metal known as the "Widow's Mite." If every woman who has learned something or enjoyed somewhat through the means of the building will contribute her mite, the thank-offering will raise and equip the permanent building in a manner worthy of the cause to which it will be devoted.

THE EDITOR.

The limits of this volume have made it impossible to mention anything outside of the Woman's Building, and, owing to unavoidable delays, much that is valuable and interesting in the building itself was made ready at too late a day to receive mention here; thus New York's fine "Loan Collection" in the Woman's Building, while arranged at an early day, was classified at too late a day to receive the mention it deserves in our book.

Attention is called to the colonial loan collections of the thirteen original States, made under the direction of the Board of Lady Managers, in the rotunda of the Government Building. These contain articles of priceless value and interest.

In the northeast corner of the gallery in the Liberal Arts Building a space is devoted to woman's work. Here may be seen a stained glass memorial window by Mary Tillinghast, very beautiful in color and tender in sentiment. Miss C. E. Scott exhibits a collection of china and embroidery which should be visited by all persons who are interested in these branches of decorative art. Annie Leota Way exhibits some clever designs, and a well-constructed relief map of Palestine, and Ella Cogswell Ripley shows some excellent designs for wall papers. These are but a few of the interesting features of this department. This section of the Liberal Arts Building is under the direction of Mrs. Rosine Ryan.—ED.